OECD ECONOMIC SURVEYS

UNITED KINGDOM

JULY 1987

ORGANISATION FOR ECONOMIC CO-OPERATION AND DEVELOPMENT

Pursuant to article 1 of the Convention signed in Paris on 14th December, 1960, and which came into force on 30th September, 1961, the Organisation for Economic Co-operation and Development (OECD) shall promote policies designed:

- to achieve the highest sustainable economic growth and employment and a rising standard of living in Member countries, while maintaining financial stability, and thus to contribute to the development of the world economy;
- to contribute to sound economic expansion in Member as well as non-member countries in the process of economic development; and
- to contribute to the expansion of world trade on a multilateral, non-discriminatory basis in accordance with international obligations.

The original Member countries of the OECD are Austria, Belgium, Canada, Denmark, France, the Federal Republic of Germany, Greece, Iceland, Ireland, Italy, Luxembourg, the Netherlands, Norway, Portugal, Spain, Sweden, Switzerland, Turkey, the United Kingdom and the United States. The following countries became Members subsequently through accession at the dates indicated hereafter: Japan (28th April, 1964), Finland (28th January, 1969), Australia (7th June, 1971) and New Zealand (29th May, 1973).

The Socialist Federal Republic of Yugoslavia takes part in some of the work of the OECD (agreement of 28th October, 1961).

Publié également en français.

CONTENTS

TABLES

3

DIAGRAMS

BASIC STATISTICS OF THE UNITED KINGDOM

THE LAND

Area (1 000 sq. km)	241	Major cities (population in millions, 1985 mid-year estimates):	
Agricultural area (1 000 sq. km), 1985	187		
		Greater London	6.8
		Birmingham	1.0
		Glasgow	0.7
		Leeds	0.7
		Sheffield	0.5

THE PEOPLE

Population (30.6.1985)	56 618 000	Total civilian employment, 1986	24 239 000
No. inhabitants per sq. km	235	*of which:*	
Net increase in population, 1980-1985, annual average	60 800	Agriculture	619 000
		Industry (incl. construction)	7 529 000
Percentage change at annual rate, 1980-1985	0.1	Other activities	16 091 000

THE GOVERNMENT

Public current expenditure on goods and services 1986 (per cent of GDP)	21	Composition of House of Commons, June 1987 (No. of seats):	
Public sector current receipts, 1986 (per cent of GDP)	41	Conservative	375
National debt, 31st March 1986 (ratio to General Government revenue)	109	Labour	229
		Liberal	17
		Social Democratic Party	5
		Scottish National Party	3
		Plaid Cymru	3
		Others	18
			650

Last general election: 11.6.1987

FOREIGN TRADE

Exports:		Imports:	
Exports of goods and services as a percentage of GDP (1986)	26	Imports of goods and services as a percentage of GDP (1986)	27
Main exports (percentage of total exports in 1986):		Main imports (percentage of total imports in 1986):	
Machinery	19	Machinery	19
Petroleum and petroleum products	9	Petroleum and petroleum products	6
Chemicals	10	Chemicals	7
Transport equipment	7	Non-ferrous metals	3
Textiles	2	Meat	2
Non-ferrous metals	2		
Iron and steel	2		

THE CURRENCY

Monetary unit: Pound sterling		Currency unit per US $, average of daily figures:	
		Year 1986	0.6822
		June 1987	0.6172

Note: An international comparison of certain basic statistics is given in an annex table.

INTRODUCTION

The United Kingdom is enjoying continued expansion. In spite of the importance of North Sea oil, the economy has coped better with the impact of lower oil prices than many others in the OECD area. Output growth in 1987 is likely to exceed that for most other Member countries. Recent developments also compare favourably with the generally disappointing long-term performance of the United Kingdom (Part IV), characterised by a decline in per capita income relative to other industrial countries. Measured from the previous cyclical peak in 1979, performance is less impressive, with manufacturing output still a little lower and GDP growth broadly in line with the European Community average. This reflects output losses in the initial years of the Government's medium-term-oriented strategy, which successfully reduced inflation, though accompanied by a strong rise in unemployment. Since then the strategy has been largely maintained and implemented flexibly. The policy approach appears to have contributed to the favourable recent performance which is reviewed in Part I.

After slowing down in the second half of 1985, due mainly to weaker foreign demand, activity growth reaccelerated in the course of 1986, with consumer demand boosted by strong real income gains. More recently, there has been a sharp revival in export growth, assisted by the depreciation of the pound sterling since mid-1985. Unemployment has declined since mid-1986, helped by labour market measures. Inflation dropped following the oil price fall but has picked up since then, reflecting the marked decline in the exchange rate through 1986. Wage increases have remained high but their inflationary impact has been damped by the cyclical acceleration of productivity growth. Largely as a result of the sharp drop in energy prices, the current external account moved from surplus in 1985 to broad balance in 1986.

As discussed in Part II, the buoyancy of government revenues has enabled the Government to achieve its long-term objective for the Public sector borrowing requirement (PSBR) sooner than would otherwise have been the case. Despite sharply lower oil revenues the authorities have been able to raise expenditure from previous plans and reduce the personal income tax rate, while setting the PSBR at only 1 per cent of GDP or 1987/88 (having achieved a PSBR ratio a little below 1 per cent in 1986/87). Monetary developments have been characterised by very rapid expansion of broad money and credit and by on-target growth of narrow money and high real interest rates. The exchange rate has also had an important role as an indicator of monetary conditions. Given the inflation differential, interest rates have tended to be higher than abroad. The Government has continued to attempt to improve the output/inflation split through microeconomic policies. Recent developments in this area include major financial market reforms, increased proceeds from the privatisation programme, personal income tax adjustments and additional labour market measures.

On the basis of these policies and the technical assumptions of unchanged oil prices and exchange rates, the growth of activity is projected to continue, albeit at diminishing rates. A revival of business fixed investment and stockbuilding is expected to partly compensate for decelerating expansion of private consumption and export demand. Unemployment should continue to decline slightly. According to OECD projections, inflation is likely to drift upwards and the current external account to move into small deficit. The strength of output growth consistent with the inflation objective in the medium term will depend much on further progress in improving supply-side conditions (Part IV), and any marked reduction in unemployment will hinge on moderation in pay settlements.

Previous Surveys have examined various issues related to the supply side of the economy, the latest focusing on the labour market. The special chapter of the current Survey (Part III) deals with the financial markets. The financial system is one of the most valuable assets of the United Kingdom economy. Dynamic and highly developed, it has maintained a role in world markets far exceeding that of the economy as a whole. Nevertheless, its leading position has been eroded in some fields. In order to improve the functioning of financial markets, the Government has taken a number of liberalisation measures, commencing with the abolition of exchange controls in 1979, and has encouraged a complete reorganisation of the Stock Exchange.

I. RECENT TRENDS

The United Kingdom's economic performance since the large oil price fall at the beginning of 1986 has compared favourably, and increasingly so, with that of the OECD area as a whole. At first glance, this seems rather surprising as the vast majority of OECD countries has experienced a terms-of-trade gain in real income equivalent, on average, to nearly 1 per cent of GNP while the United Kingdom has suffered a terms-of-trade related loss in real income of a similar order of magnitude. For the OECD area, the short-run net impact on activity of the shift in relative prices is estimated to have been slightly negative, because the resulting fall in oil producers' imports from OECD countries outweighed the lagged extra-domestic spending. In the case of the United Kingdom, the weakness of export markets has been felt less as the fall in the exchange rate has improved competitiveness, and business and consumer confidence have not suffered from deteriorating export expectations. Taken together, the income losers — oil companies and the Government — have, so far, broadly maintained spending while the gainers — households and non-oil companies — have increased theirs. The other side of the coin has been the elimination of the current account surplus and higher inflation than abroad. The former reflects above all the oil price fall, while the latter was the result of both exchange rate developments and higher wage increases.

Demand and output

After a period of hesitation towards the end of 1985, overall economic activity accelerated sharply through 1986 and into 1987. Real GDP (average measure) is estimated to have grown at an annual rate of 5 per cent in the first quarter of this year, exceeding its cyclical trough in 1981 by some 18 per cent. Taking 1986 as a whole, real GDP growth may have been almost 3 per cent (or $2\frac{1}{2}$ per cent if allowance is made for the direct effects of the 1984-85 coal dispute). Output of service industries increased by nearly 4 per cent, about the same as energy output. Manufacturing output grew by less than 1 per cent but picked up sharply through the year (Table 1). After a weather-induced set-back in early 1987, the recovery appears to have resumed. Given the very slow rise in the net capital stock in manufacturing, which contrasts with developments in the services and energy sectors, capacity utilisation has increased; survey indicators are now higher than in 1979 but still much lower than the cyclical peak of 1973. The main contribution to growth in 1986 came from *private consumption* (Diagram 1). Consumer spending was supported by both a strong rise in real incomes and a continued fall in the saving ratio (Table 1). The acceleration in the growth of real disposable income of households reflected sustained growth of nominal earnings and a lower rate of inflation. The fall in the saving ratio by 4 percentage points since 1980 has occurred despite relatively rapid expansion of incomes and high real interest rates, suggesting that positive wealth effects of disinflation have apparently been the overriding influence. Expenditure on durables grew by 9 per cent in 1986, twice as fast as total consumer spending. Growth of private consumption

9

Table 1. **Demand and output**

Percentage volume changes, 1980 prices, seasonally adjusted annual rates

	1981	1982	1983	1984	1985	1986	1985 I	1985 II	1986 I	1986 II
Private consumption	0.0	0.8	3.9	2.1	3.6	4.7	3.9	5.0	4.4	5.1
Government consumption	0.2	1.1	2.0	0.7	0.2	1.2	–0.3	–0.1	0.4	3.9
Gross fixed investment	–9.4	4.1	5.9	9.0	1.8	0.6	1.7	–2.2	2.2	0.2
of which:										
Public[1]	–16.7	–1.8	18.7	0.3	–14.3	1.9	–24.4	0.4	9.0	–9.5
Private residential	–10.8	0.1	11.3	8.9	–3.0	13.2	–7.6	5.6	10.0	27.7
Private non-residential	–5.3	7.8	–0.6	13.3	10.1	–2.6	16.2	–4.7	–1.7	–2.2
Final domestic demand	–1.7	1.4	3.8	3.0	2.6	3.2	2.6	2.6	3.2	4.0
Stockbuilding[2]	0.2	0.6	0.8	–0.3	0.3	0.0	0.4	–0.4	0.3	–0.3
Total domestic demand	–1.5	2.0	4.6	2.7	2.8	3.2	3.0	2.2	3.5	3.6
Exports	–0.6	0.9	2.2	6.9	5.8	3.0	7.2	–1.5	1.2	11.2
Imports	–2.5	5.5	5.5	9.2	3.1	5.8	–1.2	1.8	2.0	18.1
Foreign balance[2]	0.5	–1.1	–0.8	–0.6	0.8	–0.8	2.4	–0.9	–0.2	–1.7
Compromise adjustment[2][3]	–0.3	0.6	–0.3	0.8	–0.1	0.3	–0.9	0.6	–0.6	1.7
GDP at market prices[4]	–1.3	1.4	3.4	3.0	3.5	2.7	4.5	1.9	2.6	3.5
Memorandum items:										
Manufacturing production	–6.0	0.2	2.8	3.9	3.1	0.8	4.7	–0.5	–1.1	6.0
Employment	–3.4	–1.9	–0.5	1.7	1.4	0.5	1.6	0.7	0.3	0.9
Unemployment rate[5]	9.6	11.0	11.6	11.5	11.7	11.8	11.7	11.6	11.9	11.7
Real personal disposable income	–1.9	0.1	2.4	2.7	2.7	4.3	0.9	4.0	4.9	3.3
Saving ratio	13.4	12.9	11.6	12.1	11.4	11.0	11.6	11.2	11.4	10.6

1. General government and public corporations. Figures are affected by the privatisation programme.
2. Change as a percentage of GDP in the previous period.
3. The difference between expenditure-based GDP and «compromise» GDP. The latter is the average of the output, expenditure and income measures of GDP.
4. «Compromise» GDP. Figures for 1984 and 1985 are affected by the miners' dispute.
5. Including school-leavers.
Sources: United Kingdom National Accounts 1986 and Economic Trends.

seems to have decelerated in recent months, apparently mainly as a result of a recovery in the saving ratio. Even so, consumer spending in the first quarter of 1987 was running some $3\frac{1}{2}$ per cent above its level of a year earlier. *Public consumption*, which had virtually stagnated in real terms in 1985, increasingly contributed to GDP growth in the course of 1986 (Table 1, Diagram 1).

Fixed capital formation increased by less than 1 per cent in 1986, representing the weakest performance since 1981 (Table 1). Residential construction has, however, experienced a marked recovery from its depressed level in 1985 when it seemed to have been damped by unexpected increases in prices and interest rates. The weakness of private non-residential investment reflected only in part the reduction of North Sea oil investment. Non-oil business investment, too, failed to recover, despite a further improvement in profits (while total profits fell by $7\frac{1}{2}$ per cent, those of non-oil companies rose by 14 per cent). To some extent, the sluggish investment performance can be explained by changes in taxation. The 1984 corporate tax reform provided a strong inducement to accelerate the implementation of investment programmes. Moreover, the recent weakness of manufacturing investment included a sharp fall in the contribution of leasing, following the abolition of first-year allowances from April 1986. According to provisional estimates, business investment

Diagram 1. **Contributions to changes in real GDP**

Year-on-year percentage changes

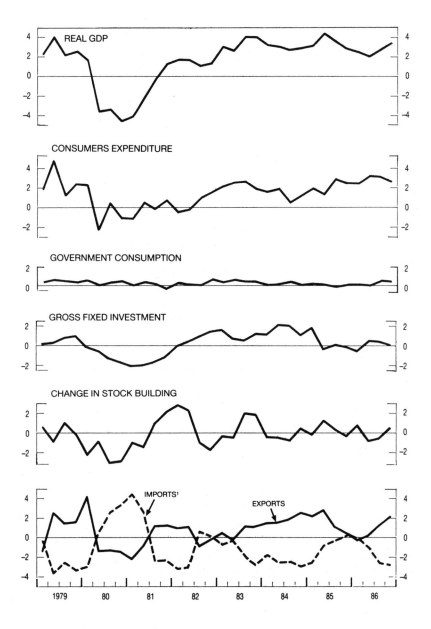

1. Inverted rates of growth.
Source: Economic Trends.

remained depressed in the first quarter of 1987. *Stockbuilding* fell in 1986. This appears to have been a consequence of both the strength of consumer demand and the trend decline of the stock/output ratio in the past few years, probably reflecting, among other things, the high cost of holding stocks and improved technology of inventory management.

While the growth of total domestic demand was relatively stable through 1986, *foreign demand* remained depressed in the early part of the year, reflecting slowing export market growth and the lagged effects of the appreciation of sterling until mid-1985. Following a reversal of these trends, exports picked up sharply (Table 1). Import growth, however, accelerated even more so that the real foreign balance acted as a drag on production. In 1986 as a whole, the fall in net exports reduced GDP growth by $^3/_4$ percentage points, after a positive growth contribution of the same size in the year before. More recently, import demand has weakened, due partly to less buoyant domestic demand, and the deterioration in the real foreign balance has been sharply reversed.

The labour market

Following a marked decline in the early 1980s, *employment* grew rapidly in the two years to mid-1985 (Table 2). Reflecting the pattern of activity growth, its rate of increase fell in the latter part of 1985 but reaccelerated through 1986. The rise in self-employment, being encouraged by various schemes and tax changes, accounts for a little under one-half of the more than 1 million jobs created since 1983. More recently, the number of self-employed has grown more slowly, though still faster than dependent employment. Rising demand for labour

Table 2. **Labour market**

Percentage changes from previous period, seasonally adjusted annual rates

| | 1981 | 1982 | 1983 | 1984 | 1985 | 1986 | 1986 | | | |
							Q1	Q2	Q3	Q4
Working population[1]	−0.1	−0.3	0.2	1.6	1.7	0.7	1.1	0.9	−0.2	0.3
Employment, total	−3.4	−1.9	−0.5	1.8	1.5	0.5	0.1	0.3	0.9	1.5
of which:										
Manufacturing	−9.0	−6.0	−5.2	−1.5	−0.3	−1.7	−2.0	−3.0	−3.5	−0.5
Employees	−4.2	−2.3	−1.0	0.8	1.2	0.5	0	0.3	0.5	1.3
of which:										
Government	−0.7	−0.9	0.5	0.1	0.4	0.4	0.8	0.6	0.2	0
Self-employed	4.8	2.6	4.7	10.6	4.2	1.5	0.6	0.6	4.0	3.8
Productivity[2]										
Total	1.9	3.8	3.9	1.5	2.1	2.4	1.8	3.9	4.9	1.0
Manufacturing	3.5	6.6	8.5	5.4	3.3	2.5	−1.8	6.8	9.0	9.6
Numbers unemployed[3]	2 270	2 626	2 866	2 998	3 113	3 180	3 176	3 203	3 202	3 140
Unemployment rate										
Excluding school-leavers	8.5	9.8	10.8	11.1	11.3	11.5	11.4	11.5	11.5	11.5
Including school-leavers	9.6	11.0	11.6	11.5	11.6	11.8	11.9	12.0	11.8	11.5
Unfilled vacancies[4]	91	114	137	150	162	189	167	176	200	213

1. All figures relate to the United Kingdom. The working population is the sum of employees in employment, the self-employed, HM Forces and the unemployed.
2. Output per person employed. Based on output-based GDP and the index of output of manufacturing industries.
3. Thousands, excluding school-leavers, on the basis of claimants rather than registration since November 1982. From April 1983, the figures were reduced by the effects of the provisions in the Budget (about 160 000 or 0.6 per cent of the labour force). See Annex III in the January 1984 OECD *Economic Survey of the United Kingdom.*
4. Thousands, excluding Community Programme vacancies.
Source: Employment Gazette.

has had a more-than-proportionate effect on part-time workers; their share in total employment is approaching one-quarter. Dependent employment in the service sector has exhibited strong buoyancy, exceeding in 1986 its previous cyclical peak of 1979 by about 7 per cent. By contrast, the decline in manufacturing employment has continued, but slowed down markedly in more recent months.

Reflecting both demographic factors and a substantial increase in female participation rates, the *labour force* has expanded strongly in 1984-85. Since then, its growth has decelerated markedly and appears to have virtually stopped rising more recently (Table 2). With employment growth picking up, the rate of *unemployment* began to fall. By May 1987, the seasonally-adjusted total of adult unemployment had dropped for the tenth consecutive month, to slightly under 3 million or just above $10^1/_2$ per cent of the total labour force, back to its 1983 level. The fall from its peak in June 1986 by almost 260 000, or about 1 per cent of the labour force, can only be partly ascribed to greater strength of activity. In fact, part seems to reflect the effects of specific government programmes. In July 1986, a new scheme for the long-term unemployed, the Restart Programme, was introduced on a national basis. From then to March 1987 most of the 1.3 million long-term unemployed had been interviewed, and about 70 000 had joined Restart training courses. By early January, about 165 000 of them had ceased claiming benefits . It is not known what proportion of those leaving the count did so as a consequence of Restart, but about 20 000 had been directed into the Community Programme and a similar number into various other schemes. In total, the Community Programme, which provides jobs for long-term unemployed adults, was covering about 240 000 people compared with 210 000 a year earlier. The coverage of the Youth Training Scheme, too, has been considerably expanded (by more than 50 000 to about 300 000 in the twelve months to April 1987). The impact of this Scheme is primarily on school-leavers rather than adult unemployment. These programmes have not only curbed the rise in registered unemployment but also substantially modified its structure: the share of young unemployed (under 25) in total unemployment has continued to fall markedly, to about one-third, and the number of long-term unemployed has started to decline.

Costs and prices

The persistence of high unemployment has not yet resulted in any significant moderation in wage growth. A remarkable feature has been the stickiness of wage trends since unemployment has stopped rising, often attributed to various hypothetical causes of hysteresis in the natural rate of unemployment such as insider-outsider theories or efficiency wage theories (see the January 1986 Survey). The underlying annual rate of growth of average earnings is estimated to have remained virtually unchanged at $7^1/_2$ per cent since mid-1984, in spite of substantial fluctuations in inflation and output. Earnings in the manufacturing sector have shown greater variations, apparently reflecting sharper changes in output growth, but their underlying rate of growth has nonetheless remained within a narrow range. Pay settlements have reacted, with a lag, to changing inflation trends. Their median annual rate fell from 6 per cent to 5 per cent through 1986, stabilising thereafter. Yet, this slowdown was offset by higher wagedrift in response to accelerating output growth in the latter part of 1986, so that the rate of growth of earnings at the turn of the year was not much different from that a year before (Table 3). The apparent inertia of wage trends conceals, however, very different developments, in particular within the service sector. Average earnings in banking, finance and insurance, and in education and health services have grown at annual rates of around 10 per cent in recent months, representing a continuation of previous trends in the financial service sector and the effect of some important settlements in the public sector.

13

Table 3. **Costs and prices**

Percentage changes from the same period a year earlier

	1982	1983	1984	1985	1986	1986				1987
						Q1	Q2	Q3	Q4	Q1
Retail prices	8.6	4.6	5.0	6.1	3.4	4.2	2.5	3.0	3.7	3.9
Producer prices[1]										
Materials and fuel purchased	7.3	6.9	8.1	1.6	-8.1	-9.5	-9.3	-9.3	-3.9	-1.8
Output home sales	7.8	5.4	6.2	5.5	4.5	5.0	4.5	4.4	4.2	4.1
Import prices[2]	6.4	7.9	9.1	3.6	-3.5	-7.1	-6.3	-2.5	2.1	
of which:[3]										
Goods	7.9	9.3	9.6	3.9	-7.7	-9.6	-11.6	-7.9	-0.9	1.7
Non-oil goods	7.1	10.2	9.6	4.1	-0.2	-4.8	-3.9	0.9	7.3	5.7
Earnings and wages										
Average earnings	9.4	8.4	6.1	8.5	7.9	8.3	8.1	7.4	7.9	7.3
Manufacturing	11.2	9.0	8.7	9.1	7.6	7.9	7.5	7.2	8.0	7.9
Public administration	8.0	6.8	6.6	6.1	5.6	4.6	6.2	5.4	6.2	
Memorandum items:										
National accounts deflators										
Private consumption	8.7	5.0	4.8	5.4	3.7	4.6	3.8	3.5	3.0	
GDP at market prices	7.7	5.1	4.0	6.1	3.7	5.5	3.7	3.4	2.4	
New house prices	2.0	11.5	7.8	8.8	17.6	13.1	18.7	20.4	16.0	17.5
Unit wage costs[4]										
Total	5.8	4.5	4.1	5.2	5.3	6.0	6.1	4.3	5.2	
Manufacturing	4.3	0.4	3.1	5.7	5.1	7.9	6.9	3.5	2.1	1.2

1. Manufacturing industries.
2. Goods and services, average values.
3. Balance of payments basis.
4. Wages and salaries per unit of output.
Sources: Employment Gazette and *Economic Trends.*

Given fairly steady wage growth, variations in unit labour cost increases have reflected primarily changes in productivity growth. Mirroring output developments, these have been particularly pronounced in manufacturing. As a result, the growth of unit wage costs in this sector accelerated from early 1984 to reach an annual rate of about 8 per cent in early 1986, and has come down sharply since then (Table 3 and Diagram 2). In contrast, raw material and fuel prices fell markedly from mid-1985 to mid-1986 but have picked up thereafter. The combined effect of these developments has been a sharp slowdown in the growth of total unit costs in 1986, with some reacceleration in the latter part of the year and into 1987. The response of manufacturing output prices to lower cost pressures has been relatively slow (Table 3), reflecting a significant improvement in profit margins. The rate of growth of the GDP deflator fell, however, much more in 1986 than that of overall unit labour costs, as a result of the oil sector's falling prices and profits. The year-on-year increase in the retail price index decelerated from 7 per cent in mid-1985 to 2½ per cent in mid-1986 but had climbed up to more than 4 per cent by May 1987. Excluding mortgage interest rates and seasonal food, both the slowdown (from 5½ per cent to 3 per cent) and the reacceleration (to 3¾ per cent) were much less pronounced. One area, however, where price increases have accelerated sharply is housing: the rise in house prices has doubled since 1985 and shows little sign of abating (Table 3).

Diagram 2. **Wages, productivity, and unit wage costs**

Year-on-year percentage changes

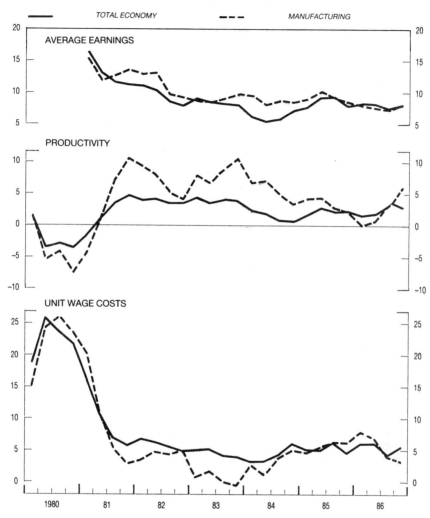

——— TOTAL ECONOMY   – – – MANUFACTURING

AVERAGE EARNINGS

PRODUCTIVITY

UNIT WAGE COSTS

Source: Economic Trends.

External balance

Recent balance-of-payments developments have been influenced by two major events: the steep decline in the oil price during the first half of 1986, which was only partially reversed thereafter, and the sharp depreciation of sterling until the end of 1986. The oil price dropped by about one-half in dollar terms in 1986 as a whole and a little more in sterling terms. The effective exchange rate of sterling had risen sharply in the first half of 1985; its subsequent fall accelerated with the drop in the oil price. Some recovery has taken place more recently as a lagged response to the rebound of the oil price. In the eighteen months to end-1986, sterling depreciated by 18 per cent in nominal effective terms. Despite an appreciation of sterling by more than 5 per cent in recent months, and stronger cost increases than abroad up to early 1986, the United Kingdom's competitive position is still considerably better than two years ago (Table 4). The oil price and exchange rate changes have adversely affected the terms of trade, but improved competitiveness has already favourably influenced real export performance.

Following a marked fall after mid-1985, merchandise exports (volume) picked up sharply in the course of 1986 (Table 4). In the second half of the year, exports of manufactures grew

Table 4. **External trade and the current account**

Seasonally-adjusted figures

	1982	1983	1984	1985	1986	1986 Q1	Q2	Q3	Q4	1987 Q1
						Indices, 1980=100				
I. Volumes[1]										
Merchandise exports	101.9	103.8	112.5	118.7	123.1	117.5	121.9	122.6	130.5	130.0
of which:										
Manufactures[2]	98	96	107	116	117	112	116	118	123	122
Fuels	133	148	160	172	176	178	170	174	179	183
Non-oil	96.9	97.2	104.9	110.6	115.2	108.2	114.7	114.7	123.1	121.8
Merchandise imports	101.5	109.7	121.8	126.0	133.9	124.9	128.8	138.5	143.4	133.2
of which:										
Manufactures[2]	115	131	147	154	163	153	157	168	174	161
Fuels	75	67	87	86	93	70	85	112	106	91
Non-oil	105.9	116.4	128.2	133.0	140.5	133.8	135.1	143.5	149.5	139.7
II. Prices[3]										
Export unit values	116.2	125.7	136.0	143.5	136.6	139.0	134.8	134.3	138.1	140.7
Import unit values	116.7	127.5	139.7	145.2	134.0	137.6	131.5	130.2	137.0	140.0
						£ billion, actual rates				
Exports, fob	55.6	60.8	70.4	78.1	72.8	18.2	17.8	17.6	19.3	19.6
Imports, fob	53.2	61.6	74.8	80.3	81.1	19.4	19.3	20.4	21.9	20.8
Trade balance	2.3	−0.8	−4.4	−2.2	−8.3	−1.2	−1.5	−2.9	−2.6	−1.1
of which:										
Non-oil	−2.3	−7.8	−11.3	−10.3	−12.4	−3.1	−2.3	−3.5	−3.4	−2.3
Services, net	2.6	3.6	3.8	5.7	5.4	1.2	1.2	1.4	1.5	1.4
Interest, profits										
and dividends, net	1.0	2.4	4.4	3.4	5.1	1.2	1.1	1.5	1.3	1.2
Transfers, net	−2.0	−2.1	−2.3	−3.5	−2.3	−0.1	−0.6	−0.8	−0.8	−0.8
Invisibles, net	1.6	4.0	6.0	5.6	8.1	2.3	1.7	2.1	2.0	1.8[4]
Current balance	3.9	3.1	1.6	3.4	−0.1	1.1	0.2	−0.8	−0.6	0.7
						Indices, 1980=100				
Memorandum items:										
Effective exchange rate	99	93	89	90	83	85	86	81	77	78
Relative unit labour costs										
In national currency	101	99	102	103	106	106	105	105	105	
In common currency	99	90	88	89	83	87	87	81	76	

1. Total and non-oil volumes on a balance of payments basis; commodity breakdown on an overseas trade statistics basis.
2. Excluding erratic items defined as ships, North Sea installations, aircraft and precious stones.
3. Not seasonally adjusted.
4. Preliminary.
Sources: Economic Trends, CSO and DTI Press Notices, and OECD Secretariat estimates.

by 6 percentage points more than markets, as conventionally measured, largely recuperating the previous losses in market shares. Despite a slight volume decline in the first quarter of 1987, goods exports were 10 per cent higher than a year before. Imports picked up earlier and even more vigorously, due possibly to the less marked improvement in price competitiveness on internal markets, but declined sharply in the first quarter of 1987, reflecting subdued domestic demand. With a fall in real net exports and some terms-of-trade loss, the non-oil trade balance deteriorated in 1986 (Table 4). Two-thirds of the £6 billion increase in the trade deficit was, however, accounted for by the fall in the net oil surplus (Diagram 3). Reflecting above all the sharp decline in import volumes, but also a reversal in the deterioration in the terms of trade, the trade deficit dropped markedly in the first quarter of 1987, back to the level of a year earlier.

Diagram 3.   **Current account developments**

£ billion

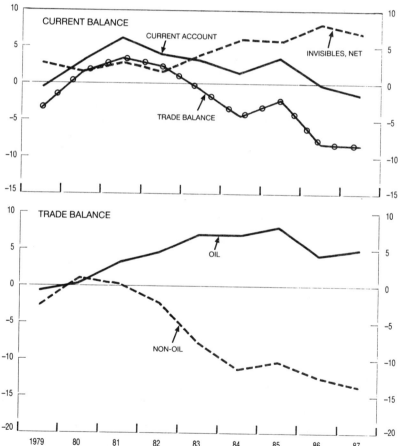

Sources: Economic Trends and OECD projections.

The current account surplus in the first half of the 1980s was attributable to the rising oil surplus which reached a peak of £8 billion in 1985 (Diagram 3). Excluding oil, the current external balance turned into deficit in the early phase of the recovery. The rising surplus on invisibles, reflecting above all buoyant investment income and exports of financial services, has helped, however, to limit the widening of the non-oil current deficit. In 1986, the deterioration in the current account largely reflected the adverse effect of the oil price fall. The current account was in broad balance in the year as a whole, following a surplus of £3½ billion in 1985. The favourable trends of merchandise trade recorded during the first four months of this year suggest that the current account has switched back into surplus.

II. THE POLICY ENVIRONMENT

Previous Surveys have discussed the origins and evolution of the Government's medium-term-oriented economic strategy. Its twofold objective has been to bring down inflation — and ultimately to achieve price stability — through macroeconomic policies, and to improve the output responsiveness of the economy through microeconomic policies. Originally the inflation target was to be achieved by a progressive reduction in the money stock growth, accompanied by a decline in public borrowing to avoid excessive upward pressures on interest rates. Since 1982, nominal income growth has been explicitly included in the projections of the Medium Term Financial Strategy (MTFS), which was launched in the 1980 Budget. While considerable progress has been made in achieving ultimate objectives, it has proved more difficult to meet some of the intermediate targets (Table 5). The conduct of monetary policy has been particularly difficult, as the information content of most monetary aggregates about conditions in the economy has been persistently blurred by the effects of deregulation and innovation in financial markets.

Fiscal policy

Since its inception in 1980, the MTFS has aimed at a steady decline of the Public Sector Borrowing Requirement (PSBR) as a percentage of GDP (Table 5). The 1984 Green Paper which discussed appropriate fiscal policies over the longer term assumed that the PSBR/GDP ratio would be brought down to 1 per cent by the 1990s. Given the unexpected buoyancy of non-oil revenues and the acceleration of the privatisation programme, this objective was achieved in 1986/87. Both the public sector and general government financial deficits (which exclude financial transactions) have fallen rather less as a share of GDP to a little below 3 per cent (Diagram 4), which is close to the OECD average. The gross government debt/GDP ratio has shown some decline over the past six years or so but at about 50 per cent has remained relatively high by international comparison.

With public sector borrowing at a low level, curbing public spending provides relatively greater scope for tax reductions. The marked rise in the tax/GDP ratio which took place in the early 1980s has so far been reversed only partially. The personal income tax burden has been reduced to the 1979 level while corporate tax receipts have risen sharply in recent years (see below). Total government revenue is still higher in relation to GDP than at the end of the 1970s despite recent declines in oil revenue (Diagram 4). As to government spending, developments in recent years have fallen short of plans. Nevertheless, at an annual rate of less than 2 per cent, real growth of public spending (national accounts definition) in the 1980s has been significantly lower than previously. The ratio of government expenditure to GDP has declined since 1984 (Diagram 4) and it is planned to come down to the 1979 level by 1988.

The authorities faced a difficult decision in the Budget of 1986 whether to stick to previous borrowing targets or not. On the one hand, the halving in North Sea revenues might have pointed to some increase in public borrowing relative to the previous MTFS. On the

Table 5. **The Medium term Financial Strategy; projections and outturns**[1]

	1979/80	1980/81	1981/82	1982/83	1983/84	1984/85	1985/86	1986/87	1987/88	1988/89	1989/90	1990/91
Money supply: sterling M3 (per cent change)												
June 1979[2]	*7-11*											
March 1980	—	*7-11*	6-10	5-9	4-8	—	—	—	—	—	—	—
March 1981	—	—	*6-10*	5-9	4-8	—	—	—	—	—	—	—
March 1982	—	—	—	*8-12*	7-11	6-10	—	—	—	—	—	—
March 1983	—	—	—	—	*7-11*	6-10	5-9	—	—	—	—	—
March 1984	—	—	—	—	—	*6-10*	5-9	4-8	3-7	2-6	—	—
March 1985	—	—	—	—	—	—	*5-9*[3]	4-8	3-7	2-6	—	—
March 1986	—	—	—	—	—	—	—	*11-15*[4]	—	—	—	—
Actual[5]	16.2	19.4	12.8	11.2	9.4	11.9	16.9	19.0	—	—	—	—
Money supply: M0 (per cent change)												
March 1984	—	—	—	—	—	*4-8*	3-7	2-6	1-5	0-4	—	—
March 1985	—	—	—	—	—	—	*3-7*	2-6	1-5	0-4	—	—
March 1986	—	—	—	—	—	—	—	*2-6*	2-6	1-5	1-5	—
March 1987	—	—	—	—	—	—	—	—	*2-6*	1-5	1-5	0-4
Actual[6]	10.0	6.5	0	6.4	4.8	5.4	4.1	3.5	—	—	—	—
Public sector borrowing requirement (per cent of GDP)												
June 1979	*4½*											
March 1980	4¾	*3¾*	3	2¼	1½	—	—	—	—	—	—	—
March 1981	5	6	*4¼*	3¼	2	—	—	—	—	—	—	—
March 1982	—	5.7	4¼	*3½*	2¾	2	—	—	—	—	—	—
March 1983	—	—	3½	2¾	*2¾*	2½	2	—	—	—	—	—
March 1984	—	—	—	3.3	3¼	*2¼*	2	2	1¾	1¾	—	—
March 1985	—	—	—	—	3.2	3¼	2	2	1¾	1¾	—	—
March 1986	—	—	—	—	—	3.1	2	*1¾*	1¾	1½	1½	—
March 1987	—	—	—	—	—	—	1.6	1	*1*	1	1	1
Actual	4.8	5.6	3.4	3.2	3.2	3.1	1.6	0.9[7]	—	—	—	—
Actual (£ billion)	10.0	12.7	8.6	8.9	9.8	10.2	5.8	3.3	—	—	—	—

1. Figures in italics are targets.
2. A target for the ten months to April 1980 was published in the June 1979 Budget.
3. The 5 to 9 per cent target for the growth of sterling M3 in 1985/86 was abandoned on 17th October 1985.
4. The illustrative ranges of growth of sterling M3 for later years were not published in the March 1986 Budget. There was no formal target for sterling M3 in the March 1987 Budget.
5. Seasonally adjusted annualised rates for relevant periods stated in the June 1979 Budget and in successive MTFS.
6. March to March.
7. Based on OECD estimate for GDP in the first quarter of calendar 1987.

Sources: *Financial Statement and Budget Reports*, 1979-80 to 1987-88, and *Financial Statistics*.

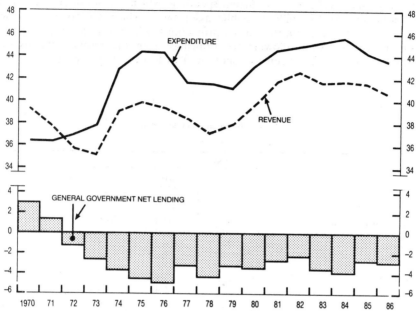

Diagram 4. **General government revenue and expenditure**
Per cent of GDP

Source: *United Kingdom National Accounts, 1986.*

other hand, given the increase in planned privatisation proceeds, which are essentially transitory, there was a case for a reduction in the borrowing requirement. In the event, the authorities decided to broadly adhere to the targets set prior to the oil price fall. In view of the better-than-expected outcome for 1985/86 (Table 6), the PSBR for 1986/87 was set at about £7 billion, less than 2 per cent of GDP and somewhat lower than indicated in the 1985 MTFS. This target was to be achieved by a combination of increased public asset sales, more prudent tax reductions and higher non-oil revenues than previously envisaged.

According to provisional estimates, the PSBR for 1986/87 was less than half of that envisaged in the initial budget and about £2½ billion below that for the year before (Table 6). In relation to GDP it was the lowest since 1969/70 (and even excluding privatisation proceeds, it was lower than in any year since 1971/72). This favourable outcome was achieved in spite of a sharper-than-expected fall in oil *revenues* (by almost £7 billion). Other tax revenues were much higher than forecast, with non-North Sea corporation tax accounting for the bulk of the additional receipts. The reasons for this surge in corporate taxes are not fully understood, as the recorded rise in profits would seem to be insufficient to explain the outcome and may be too low. It may also be that several years of rising profits, perhaps combined with the effects of changes to the system of investment allowances introduced in the 1984 Budget, have led to a situation where a substantial number of companies have crossed from being tax-exhausted to tax paying. The greater-than-expected buoyancy of indirect taxes reflects both stronger-than-forecast consumer spending and a change in the composition of consumption towards spending on goods and services subject to VAT. The sharp rise in stamp duties is attributable to a rapidly expanding securities turnover and rising securities and house prices.

21

An improvement in the financial position of public corporations also helped to bring down the PSBR in 1986/87. On the *expenditure side,* there was considerable overspending in the areas of social security and local authority current spending, which are not directly controlled by central government. At £4¼ billion, public asset sales, which are counted as negative expenditure, appear to have almost met the projections, which were for a near doubling of privatisation proceeds. After allowing for drawings from the reserve, the expenditure planning total seems to have been overshot by a little over ½ per cent.

Table 6.   **Budgetary developments**

£ billion

	1985/86	1986/87			1987/88
	Outturn	Budget forecast	Outturn[1]		Budget forecast
Receipts					
Taxes on income and oil royalties	54.2	52.8	53.1		56.6
Taxes on expenditure	57.8	61.9	63.5		67.8
National insurance	24.7	26.2	26.5		28.5
Gross trading surplus	8.3	7.4	7.1		7.1
Rent, etc.	3.8	3.8	3.8		3.9
Interest and dividends	4.7	4.8	4.1		4.2
Other items[2]	4.8	5.4	5.3		6.1
Total	*158.3*	*162.2*	*163.5*		*174.2*
Expenditure					
Final consumption[3]	75.3	77.6	80.7		85.1
Subsidies	7.2	6.7	6.3		6.1
Current grants	49.8	51.6	54.2		55.3
Debt interest	18.3	18.7	18.3		18.7
Investment	12.7	12.2	12.3		11.6
Other capital items[4]	3.4	3.0	2.8		3.2
Unallocated items[5]	—	4.5	—		3.5
Total	*166.7*	*174.4*	*174.5*		*183.6*
Financial deficit	*8.4*	*12.2*	*11.0*		*9.4*
Lending to private sector and abroad	0.2	—	—		–0.2
Cash expenditure on company securities, net[6]	2.8	4.8	4.0		5.0
Pension transactions	0.7	0.6	0.8		0.5
Accruals adjustment	–0.8	–0.1	0.1		—
Miscellaneous financial transactions	–0.3	–0.3	2.0		0.2
Borrowing requirement (PSBR)[7]	*5.8*	*7.1*	*4.1*	*(3.3)*	*3.9*
of which:					
Central government	4.1		5.0	(4.6)	
Local authorities	1.7		0.5	(0.1)	
Public corporations	0		–1.4	(–1.4)	

1. Preliminary (March 1987 Budget).
2. Imputed charge for non-trading capital consumption, taxes on capital and capital transfers from private sector.
3. Includes non-trading capital consumption.
4. Increase in stocks plus capital grants to private sector.
5. Refers for 1986/87 and 1987/88 to projected contingency reserve.
6. Inclunding privatisation proceeds.
7. Adjusted for lending within public sector. Latest available figures for the outturn in 1986/87 (Press Notice CSO(87)36. 17/4/1987) are in brackets.
Sources: Financial Statement and Budget Reports 1986-87 and 1987-88, and *Financial Statistics.*

In his 1986 Autumn Statement, the Chancellor announced an increase in the 1987/88 public expenditure planning total by £4¾ billion representing a rise of more than 3 per cent compared with its previous target. Privatisation proceeds were envisaged to be raised to £5 billion and the reserve to be lowered to £3½ billion. The PSBR target of £7 billion was confirmed. The March 1987 Budget decision to set public borrowing at about the expected favourable outturn for 1986/87 of £4 billion limited the room for tax adjustments to about the amount foreshadowed in the 1986 MTFS. The basic rate of personal income tax has been cut by 2 points to 27 per cent following a 1 per cent cut in 1986. The corporation tax rate for small companies has been reduced accordingly while the main corporate rate remains unchanged at 35 per cent. Spending plans are unchanged from those in the Autumn Statement and Public Expenditure White Paper, which raised previous projections for local authority and social security expenditure, in particular. While the oil price assumption of $15 per barrel underlying the revenues estimates now seems very cautious, expenditure targets may be put under renewed pressure, given past experience. In particular, public sector pay could grow more than allowed for in the Budget. Hence, the reserve can be expected to be fully spent and some overshooting of the planning total could occur, although the downward trend of public spending as a proportion of GDP is likely to be continued. The scale of further tax cuts will be made dependent on the success in curbing public expenditure growth, which is planned to slow down markedly in 1988/89, but will depend also on non-North Sea revenue buoyancy. The intention is to reduce the basic rate of personal income tax to 25 per cent eventually.

Monetary policy

Maintenance of downward pressure on inflation has remained the primary objective of monetary policy. The implementation of policies has continued to be rather pragmatic, responding flexibly to unrest in international exchange markets and changes in the private sector's liquidity and portfolio behaviour. The shift of emphasis away from broad money towards other indicators, in particular the exchange rate, has become more manifest. The target for £M3, temporarily suspended in October 1985 but reinstated in the March 1986 Budget, was dropped in the 1987 MTFS. This step was recommended by the Governor of the Bank of England in his Loughborough University speech, where he argued that the relationship between the rate of growth of broad money and that of nominal incomes had become increasingly unpredictable because of the fast pace of financial innovation and liberalisation. Targeting of M0 (cash held by the private sector and the banks) is continued. The target range for narrow money growth in 1987/88 has been kept unchanged at 2 to 6 per cent. By the end of the decade a gradual reduction to a range of 0 to 4 per cent is envisaged, in line with the projected path for nominal GDP growth. Underlying growth of M0 significantly outside its target range would prompt the authorities to change short-term interest rates, unless other indicators, including broad money and the exchange rate, advised against it. The United Kingdom is a party to the Louvre Accord agreed in Paris in February which stated that a period of exchange rate stability was desirable. But that should not be taken to mean that the authorities have a fixed target range for the exchange rate which they will necessarily intervene to defend regardless of all other circumstances.

In contrast to broad money targets, those for narrow money have been met since their introduction in 1984 (Table 5). M0 accounts for about 6 per cent of the broadest aggregate (previously PSL2, now M5, see Annex II). The relationship between M0 and nominal income has been relatively stable, with the year-to-year increases of velocity staying within a range of 0 to 6 per cent. In 1986/87, M0 grew by no more than 3.5 per cent despite some acceleration prior to the rise in interest rates in October. In stark contrast has been the sharp acceleration in the rate of growth of £M3 (now redesignated M3, Table 7). Indeed, in 1986/87, it expanded

Table 7. Formation of the money supply

£ billion

| | Unadjusted | | | | | | Seasonally adjusted | | | | | |
	1984/85	1985/86	1986/87	1985 Q1	Q2	Q3	Q4	1986 Q1	Q2	Q3	Q4	1987 Q1
Public sector borrowing requirement	10.2	5.8	3.3	2.5	1.4	1.9	1.2	1.3	2.1	2.5	-2.5	1.3
Public sector debt sales[1]	-12.6	-3.5	-1.2	-4.2	-1.7	-0.8	-1.1	0.1	-0.4	-1.2	-1.8	2.2
Lending in sterling[1]	18.6	21.4	30.3	6.2	4.9	4.6	5.4	6.2	6.4	7.0	10.5	6.6
Domestic counterparts	16.2	23.6	32.4	4.5	4.6	5.6	5.5	7.6	8.1	8.3	6.2	10.1
Net external finance	-1.7	-2.5	-2.4	0.7	-0.2	-0.4	-2.6	0.8	0.9	-1.7	-2.3	1.2
Net non-deposit liabilities	-2.7	-2.0	-4.6	-1.3	-1.4	-0.5	0.1	-0.2	-2.1	-0.1	-1.3	-1.1
Sterling M3[2]	11.8	19.1	25.4	3.9	2.9	4.7	3.0	8.2	6.9	6.2	2.3	10.2
Memorandum item:												
Overfunding (-)	-4.5	0.4	0.4	-2.7	-1.1	0.7	-0.9	1.8	1.4	0.3	-5.4	4.2

1. To non-bank, non-building society private sector.
2. Sterling M3 was redesignated M3 in mid-May 1987 (see Annex II).
Source: *Bank of England Quarterly Bulletin.*

by almost 20 per cent, overshooting the target of 11 to 15 per cent by a wide margin. The decline in velocity of broad monetary measures, which commenced in 1981 and was particularly marked in 1985 and 1986, can be related to a number of factors among which financial innovation and deregulation (see Part III) as well as disinflation appear to have been the most important ones; more recently, the end of overfunding the PSBR (Table 7) has also contributed. It should be noted, however, that M3's velocity declined much more sharply than

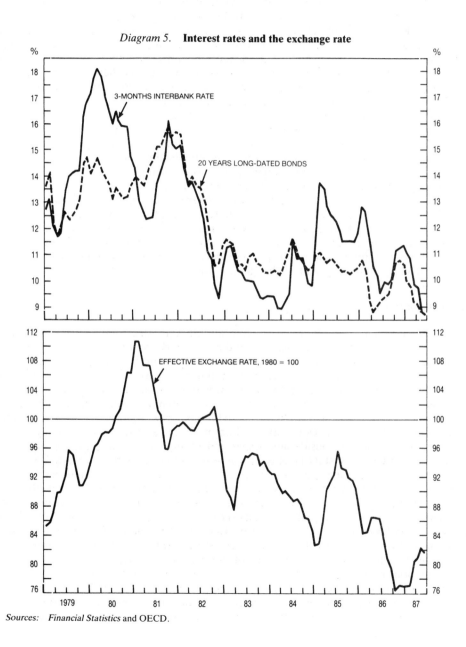

Diagram 5. **Interest rates and the exchange rate**

Sources: *Financial Statistics* and OECD.

that of other broad money measures in 1986-87. Banks successfully competed to raise their market share of deposits, especially at the expense of building societies. In addition, building societies have tended to increase the proportion of their liquid assets held as bank deposits rather than in gilts. Both factors, which raised M3 relative to other broad money measures, have little macroeconomic significance.

Given the unstable and hence unpredictable behaviour of broader monetary aggregates, other indicators have increasingly served as a guide to monetary policy. The exchange rate, in particular, has assumed a greater influence. In January and October 1986 interest rates were raised when the decline in the effective exchange rate appeared excessive (Diagram 5) and it was also warranted by domestic monetary conditions. Sterling was, nevertheless, allowed to fall in response to the oil price collapse, as the adverse impact on inflation was expected to be offset by the effects of lower oil prices. In the course of the first half of 1986, and in the context of global interest rate reductions, banks' base rates came down by $2\frac{1}{2}$ points to 10 per cent. Their renewed rise by 1 percentage point later in the year was preceded by strong downward pressures on sterling. The move out of sterling, which occurred in the face of recovering oil prices, appears to have reflected financial market concern about accelerating monetary expansion and deteriorating prospects for inflation and the balance of payments. With good news from the budgetary front and the balance-of-payments side, financial sentiment has improved and sterling appreciated more recently. Given the rapid growth in bank lending and the initially muted reaction of the exchange rate to the rising oil price, the authorities adopted a cautious approach to cuts in interest rates, though finally allowing them to fall. In the two months to early May 1987, banks' base rates were reduced in several steps to 9 per cent, the lowest level since 1984. Nonetheless, both nominal and real interest rates are still higher than generally elsewhere, reflecting the persistence of positive inflation differentials *vis-à-vis* important trading partners, and an uncertainty premium possibly related to expected greater interest and exchange rate variability.

Supply-side policies

The Government has continued to give attention to structural policies designed to promote the functioning and flexible operation of markets. Progress in the pursuit of supply-side policies was reviewed in the last two Surveys. The January 1986 Survey focused on measures affecting the labour market including a discussion of changes to industrial relations law. Part III of the present Survey deals with financial markets, where a wide range of legislative and other controls on activity have been abolished since 1979. Recent developments, other than in the financial field, comprise changes to income taxation, continued help for small businesses, tax relief on profit related pay, further employment and training measures, and a considerable expansion of the privatisation programme.

The tax and benefit system is an area where important steps have already been taken. The reform of corporate taxation announced in 1984 has now been fully implemented, with a major reduction in the tax rate and a widening of the tax base by the abolition of stock relief and advanced depreciation allowances. These changes have reduced tax distortions, making investment decisions more responsive to market signals and lessening the fiscal attraction of debt over equity financing (see Part III). A package of VAT changes to help small businesses was announced in the 1987/88 Budget. The rate of corporation tax for small companies has been reduced in line with the basic rate of personal income tax.

More ambitious measures of tax reform designed to lower the tax burden on individuals are dependent on the progress achieved in containing the growth of public expenditure. The last two budgets reduced the basic rate of personal income tax and continued to increase income tax thresholds (in real terms in 1986 and in line with inflation in 1987). A recent Green

Paper outlining the Government's proposals for the future reform of personal taxation argues that the basic rate of income tax is still too high, especially in comparison with other major industrial countries, while the tax thresholds are too low in relation to earnings. The centrepiece of the Green Paper is a proposal for the introduction of a system of fully transferable allowances between spouses. As from 1988, the introduction of family credit by the Social Security Act 1986 will provide extra financial aid for low income families with children and help to improve the replacement ratio (relative incomes in and out of work). The Act also establishes the general right (with effect from 1988) to join a personal pension scheme. Moreover, the 1987 Budget gives personal pensions the same favourable tax treatment as retirement annuities. These measures should be conducive to labour mobility.

Existing employment and training measures have been improved and expanded, and new schemes introduced, including the Restart programme for the long-term unemployed, the New Worker Scheme for young people, and the new Job Training Scheme (see Labour Market section in Part I). In real terms, government expenditure on employment, training and related measures has more than doubled since 1978/79. Following the publication of a Green Paper and discussions with employers and others, the Government announced in the 1987/88 Budget that it intended to introduce income tax relief for participants in profit related pay (PRP) schemes registered with the Inland Revenue lasting at least one year; one-half of PRP would be free of income tax up to a limit of £3 000 per year or 20 per cent of pay whichever is lower. The authorities expect that encouragement of PRP will protect jobs that may be at risk and get jobless back into work more quickly. Yet, the response of both employers and trade unions has so far been tepid. The Government has issued a Green Paper containing proposals to further strengthen the right of individual union members and improve unions' internal democracy. The authorities have also urged the abandonment of wage bargaining at the national level in favour of decentralised settlements in which local conditions would play an important role. This is expected to reduce regional differences in unemployment.

The upward momentum of the Government's privatisation programme has been maintained and is expected to yield proceeds of £5 billion per year (more than 1 per cent of GDP) over the rest of the decade. No enterprise or public utility has in principle been excluded from the scope of the programme. To date, fifteen major companies and some smaller concerns have been transferred to the private sector, involving around 650 000 employees. These transactions have reduced the state-owned sector of industry by more than one-third since 1979 (for details see Annex I). The most important so far have been the sales of British Telecom in 1984 and British Gas in 1986. The success of these flotations has contributed to wider share ownership (see Part III). Privatisations planned for the future include BAA (formerly the British Airports Authority), the Water Authorities and the electricity industry. The authorities believe that the programme will increase productive efficiency and benefit consumers. There are signs of efficiency gains within both the privatised and still nationalised sector, as a result of measures taken to prepare state-owned businesses for privatisation. Competition has, however, been introduced very cautiously for the privatised large monopolies.

III. FINANCIAL MARKETS

Introduction and overview

The United Kingdom has a long tradition as an important international financial centre. Its leading position in world financial markets is partly attributable both to its trading and imperial history and its liberal regulations on foreign trade and financial transactions. While the weight of the United Kingdom economy in world output and trade has declined and sterling's role as a trading and reserve currency has diminished, London has succeeded in maintaining its importance as an international financial centre by attracting the Eurocurrency and Eurobond markets. Nevertheless, the development of other financial centres and the trend towards greater integration of, and competition among, financial markets has tended to erode the dominant position of London in some fields.

Concern over the City's loss of international competitiveness and the conviction of the benefits of greater competition have led the present Government to take a series of liberalisation measures. The abolition of foreign exchange controls for residents in 1979 has accelerated the internationalisation of London as a financial market and opened up the domestic market to international competition. Further measures, such as the move towards a more market-oriented monetary policy and away from quantitative controls, were in a way the inevitable consequence of the first step. They have reduced domestic market segmentation and barriers between financial institutions, accelerating the trend towards financial conglomerates with wide-ranging functions. Financial reforms have culminated in the complete reorganisation of the Stock Exchange, aimed at establishing an open and fully competitive domestic and international equity market able to complement London's strong position in foreign currency trading, Eurobonds and international banking among others. The deregulation and growing internationalisation of financial markets have certainly increased competition but also the risk of losses and malpractices. Prudential controls have, therefore, been completed and tightened. Hence, the overall result of recent reforms represents a mixture of liberalisation and greater regulation of financial markets.

In order to put the financial system in a macroeconomic perspective, this Part of the Survey starts with a description of the financial sector's direct contribution to the economy, in terms of output, employment and the balance of payments, and of the pattern of financial flows between different sectors of the economy. The subsequent sections deal with London's role in world financial markets, the institutional set-up and the financial reforms of the present Government. The concluding section attempts to assess the financial system's impact on economic performance.

The financial system in a macroeconomic perspective

The financial sector's contribution to the economy

Besides their role as intermediaries between economic units and sectors wishing to borrow and lend funds, financial institutions make more tangible contributions to the economy, producing a wide range of services, generating income, creating employment opportunities and earning money from overseas through net exports of services. The output

Table 8. **Financial sector's share**

Per cent of GDP

	1970	1975	1980	1985	1970	1975	1980	1985
	Financial institutions and insurance				Including real estate and business services			
United Kingdom	..	5.9	6.3	7.4	15.0	16.5	17.7	19.7
United States	4.2	3.9	4.6	4.7	18.5	18.4	20.7	22.8
Canada					9.8	10.4	10.3	13.0[1]
Japan					12.3	13.4	14.6	15.2[1]
Germany	3.2	4.5	4.5	5.7[1]	8.2	10.4	10.3	12.2
France					13.4	14.8	16.6	18.1[1]
Italy					16.7	19.5	18.2	20.5
Switzerland[2]	3.6	4.5	5.3	6.9[1]				

1. 1984.
2. Excluding insurance.
Sources: OECD National Accounts and CSO.

of service industries, and in particular of financial institutions, is notoriously difficult to define and measure. International comparisons are particularly hazardous, as statistics are not always available for the desirable definition and grouping. But Table 8, along with additional information for smaller countries, suggests that the United Kingdom financial sector's share in total value added is among the highest in the OECD area. In 1975 the total factor incomes of the financial sector represented about 6 per cent of the total net value added in the economy, with banking and insurance accounting for about one-half and one-third, respectively, of the sector's contribution (Table 9). Since then the financial sector's share has risen to $7\frac{1}{2}$ per cent. Value added of non-bank financial institutions has grown particularly strongly. This is in large part due to the increase in finance leasing activity. In 1985, non-bank financial institutions accounted for almost one-third of the financial sector's value added.

Figures at constant prices are only available for the broader grouping of financial and business services, which includes, among other things, rapidly expanding items such as property owning and managing. Over the last decade or so real output of this sector has grown

Table 9. **Gross value added in the financial sector**

Per cent of GDP

	1975	1980	1985
Banking and bill discounting[1]	2.7	2.6	2.6
Other financial institutions	1.3	1.4	2.2
Insurance	1.9	2.3	2.7
Total financial sector	5.9	6.3	7.4
£ billion	5.6	12.6	22.6
Memorandum item:			
Banking, finance, insurance, business services			
and leasing	10.6	11.6	13.9
£ billion	10.0	23.1	42.5

1. The Banking sector definition was widened in 1982-83 into a definition of monetary sector. The effect was to move some «Other Financial Institutions» (OFIs) into the newly-defined monetary sector. Therefore, the 1985 OFIs figure is lower than it would have been on the old definition and the Banking, etc. figure is correspondingly higher, and there is a discontinuity between the relevant figures for 1980 and 1985 in this table.
Source: CSO.

by about 60 per cent while real GDP has grown by about one-fifth and manufacturing output, apart from cyclical fluctuations, has remained broadly unchanged (Diagram 6). These trends are reflected in sharply diverging employment patterns. While manufacturing employment has fallen by one-quarter, employment in financial and business services has grown by one-third and its share in total employment has risen from $6\frac{1}{2}$ per cent in the mid-1970s to more than 9 per cent. The corresponding figure for the financial sector in a narrower sense has increased by almost 1 percentage point to $3\frac{1}{2}$ per cent in 1986 (Table 10). Although the

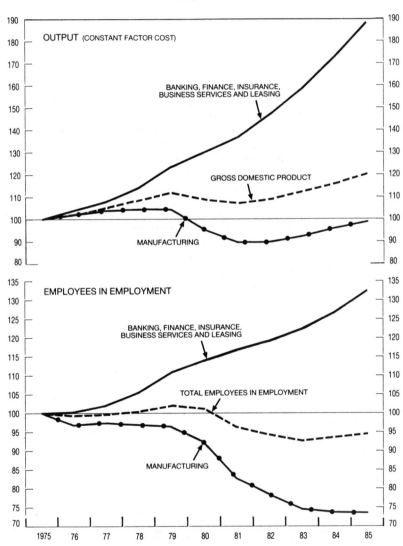

Diagram 6. **Output and employment trends**
Indices, 1975 = 100

Source: United Kingdom National Accounts, 1986.

30

Table 10. **Employment in the financial sector**

Great Britain, thousands

	Banking and bill discounting	Other financial institutions	Insurance	Total financial sector	All industries and services	Financial sector as per cent of total employment
June						
1978	335.5	89.8	202.9	628.3	22 273.5	2.8
1979	339.7	94.5	212.2	646.4	22 638.2	2.9
1980	354.4	99.7	220.1	674.2	22 458.1	3.0
1981	360.8	102.8	224.6	688.2	21 385.5	3.2
1982	362.3	105.0	219.6	686.9	20 915.5	3.3
1983	373.8	110.3	219.9	704.0	20 571.5	3.4
1984	383.6	115.7	220.7	720.0	20 741.2	3.5
1985	392.6	120.7	226.5	739.8	20 989.9	3.5
1986	399.4	127.9	231.6	758.9	21 073.2	3.6
Per cent change,						
1978-86	19.0	42.4	14.1	20.8	−5.4	—

Source: Department of Employment.

financial sector's share in total employment may appear relatively small, it is among the highest and fastest rising of Member countries. Since the mid-1970s the number of employees in the financial sector has grown by one-quarter to reach 760 000 in 1986. The share of insurance has dropped to below one-third of the total in spite of employment growth of about 2 per cent per annum in recent years. The expansion has been particularly marked in other non-bank financial institutions where the number of employees has risen by almost one-half over the last decade to reach one-sixth of total financial sector employment.

Net overseas earnings of financial institutions have made an important and growing contribution to the United Kingdom's external account balance. They consist of receipts from net exports of services to foreign residents, interest received on lending net of borrowing abroad, direct investment income (overseas profits of United Kingdom financial institutions less profits of foreign institutions operating in the United Kingdom), and portfolio investment income (on holdings of overseas securities). The insurance industry is the largest foreign exchange earner among financial institutions with net earnings of nearly £3 billion (Table 11). About one-third of this represents underwriting income, the bulk of which is earned on overseas business written in the United Kingdom by Lloyd's underwriters. The portfolio investment income of the insurance companies and Lloyd's has risen particularly fast and accounts now for almost one-half of their total earnings. Banks are next in importance to insurance with net overseas earnings of more than £2 billion. Strong growth of their income from portfolio investment and the provision of financial services has more than compensated for negative net income from both interest receipts and direct investment. Banks have moved their business away from syndicated loans to securitised lending in recent years with a consequent switch in earnings from ordinary bank interest receipts to portfolio income. This in turn is now being partially replaced by earnings from services as they move away from the direct financing of loans to underwriting and placement of customers' debt with other lenders. There has been very rapid growth in both the banks' borrowing from and lending to overseas (see below), mainly in foreign currencies. However, with interest margins small and overseas deposits in the United Kingdom exceeding lending to overseas, net interest income has become negative in recent years. Banks' earnings from their subsidiary companies and branches overseas have increasingly fallen short of those of foreign-owned banks in London

31

Table 11. **Net overseas earnings of United Kingdom financial institutions**

£ million

	1975	1976	1977	1978	1979	1980	1981	1982	1983	1984	1985
Insurance											
Credits	455	817	929	1 055	1 090	996	1 182	1 432	1 928	2 134	2 938
Debits	5	7	14	13	16	28	29	11	–34	–34	18
Net earnings	450	810	915	1 042	1 074	968	1 153	1 421	1 962	2 168	2 920
Banking											
Credits	4 356	5 203	5 497	7 113	10 522	17 035	30 057	36 851	33 514	40 590	41 532
Debits	4 349	5 085	5 514	6 798	10 730	16 875	29 157	35 863	31 958	38 275	39 478
Net earnings	7	118	–17	315	–208	160	900	988	1 556	2 315	2 054
Other investing institutions											
Net earnings	66	72	80	91	126	202	237	500	720	871	920
Stock exchange											
Net earnings	18	16	20	21	25	43	34	44	71	93	106
Total net earnings of above institutions	541	1 016	998	1 469	1 017	1 373	2 324	2 953	4 309	5 447	6 000
Total net earnings of "the City"[1]	1 029	1 524	1 441	1 987	1 611	2 020	3 139	3 862	5 418	6 660	7 130
Memorandum items:											
Current account	–1 582	–920	–136	965	–717	2 929	6 159	3 937	3 134	1 587	3 450
Visible balance	–3 333	–3 929	–2 284	–1 542	–3 449	1 361	3 360	2 331	–835	–4 384	–2 178
Invisible balance	1 751	3 009	2 148	2 507	2 732	1 568	2 799	1 606	3 969	5 971	5 628

1. Above financial institutions plus commodity trading and other brokerage, etc.
Source: United Kingdom Balance of Payments. 1986.

(see below). Among the other investing institutions, pension funds have become important foreign exchange earners as they hold a significant part of their portfolios in foreign securities.

After fluctuating around £1 billion in the second half of the 1970s, total net overseas earnings of financial institutions (excluding commodity trading and non-stock exchange brokerage) have sharply increased in the 1980s, reaching £6 billion in 1985. As a proportion of GNP, they amounted to $\frac{1}{2}$ per cent in 1975 and not much more in 1980 but reached 2 per cent in 1985. Having always been an important constituent of the invisible surplus, they have exceeded the latter in the 1980s (Table 11). But this impressive result needs to be kept in perspective. Financial services still amount to not much more than 4 per cent of total exports of goods and services, broadly unchanged from the mid-1970s, and the United Kingdom share in world exports of these services has declined (see below).

An assessment of the financial sector's contribution to the economy should include possible side effects. It has been argued that the booming financial sector has driven up the exchange rate and hence adversely affected the manufacturing sector's performance. But in this respect the development of North Sea oil has been certainly much more important. Moreover, it should be borne in mind that any successful export or import-competing firm is bound to increase competitive pressure on other sectors via the exchange rate crowding-out mechanism. Another point, often made, but carrying little weight for the same reasons, is that the City creams off the talent available within the domestic workforce and that the bidding up of salaries by City firms has adverse demonstration effects.

Although the financial sector's direct contribution to the economy in terms of output and employment has been rising, it can certainly not be expected to compensate for the shrinking of larger sectors, all the more so because capital intensity and productivity growth in the financial sector are relatively high and the increase in employment opportunities may peter out in the aftermath of its recent restructuring. However, the financial system's importance goes beyond its direct contribution to the economy. As evidenced by the growth of financial transactions, its intermediation role has increased significantly. Indicators for the extent of financial intermediation, such as the financial assets held by residents or the intermediaries' liabilities as a proportion of GDP, show a sharp rise in recent years to high levels by international comparison. This upsurge contrasts with much more moderate growth of intermediation relative to income and wealth in the preceding decades[1].

Sectoral saving/investment patterns and financial flows

A major function of the financial system is to provide an efficient channel for funds to pass from savers to investors. In recent years the United Kingdom has saved around one-fifth of GDP (Table 12), slightly down from the 1970s as generally elsewhere but much the same as in the 1950s and 1960s. Contrary to the past, saving in the economy as a whole is now close to the international average, about half way between the United States and Japan. By contrast to most other countries, gross saving by the private business sector exceeds that of the household sector. In the first half of the 1980s savings in the economy as a whole exceeded domestic investment, leading to substantial accumulation of net external assets (amounting to more than one-fifth of GDP by 1985). The swing of the saving/investment balance into sizeable surplus has closely mirrored corporate sector developments (Diagram 7). Apart from cyclical fluctuations, the United Kingdom non-financial private business sector has always been in approximate financial balance. The advent of North Sea oil and improving profitability have transformed the company sector into a significant net contributor of financial savings while the traditional positions of the household and general government sectors as net lender and net borrower, respectively, have not changed fundamentally

Table 12. **Saving and investment by sector**

Per cent of GDP

	1963-69	1970-79	1980	1981	1982	1983	1984	1985
Households								
Saving	6.3	7.8	10.6	9.2	9.0	8.0	8.3	7.7
Investment[1]	4.1	4.5	4.2	4.0	4.2	4.5	4.5	4.7
Financial balance	2.2	3.2	6.4	5.2	4.7	3.5	3.8	3.1
Private business								
Saving	7.9	10.1	7.8	7.5	7.0	8.5	10.2	9.2
Investment	7.5	9.8	7.6	6.6	6.1	6.5	7.5	7.3
Financial balance	0.4	0.4	0.2	0.9	0.9	2.0	2.7	1.9
Financial sector								
Saving	0.3	1.2	1.5	1.4	1.4	1.6	1.8	2.1
Investment	0.9	1.7	2.3	2.3	2.3	1.8	2.2	2.3
Financial balance	–0.6	–0.5	–0.8	–0.9	–0.9	–0.2	–0.4	–0.3
Public sector								
Saving	5.9	3.9	1.2	1.6	2.0	1.5	0.7	1.0
Investment	7.9	7.8	5.8	4.8	4.7	5.3	4.8	3.9
Financial balance	–2.1	–3.8	–4.6	–3.2	–2.7	–3.7	–4.1	–2.9
Domestic sectors								
Saving	20.4	23.0	21.0	19.6	19.4	19.6	21.0	20.0
Investment	20.4	23.7	19.8	17.7	17.3	18.1	19.0	18.2
Financial balance	0	–0.7	1.2	2.0	2.1	1.5	2.0	1.8
External sector								
Financial balance[2]	0.1	0.4	–1.3	–2.4	–1.4	–1.0	–0.4	–1.0
Residual error								
Financial balance	–0.1	0.3	0.1	0.3	–0.6	–0.3	–1.5	–0.9

1. Including investment of unincorporated enterprises.
2. A negative sign implies a surplus in the current account of the balance of payments.
Source: United Kingdom National Accounts, 1986.

(Table 12). The public sector's financial deficit in terms of GDP has tended to decline in the 1980s exclusively as a result of a fall in the investment share. The household sector's financial surplus has dropped markedly in recent years in relation to income, though from a historically high level in the early 1980s. The pronounced swing in the personal saving ratio appears to reflect in part structural changes in the financial system (see below). Untypically, the financial institutions have run a financial deficit, probably because they are more involved in real investment in property and in equipment leasing than elsewhere.

The flow of funds matrix in Table 13 shows the pattern of lending and borrowing which financed the sectoral surpluses and deficits. The gross flow into the financial institutions has substantially exceeded the private sector's surplus. In recent years claims on financial institutions and government debt acquired by households have been about three times their financial surplus. About half of the personal sector's additions to financial assets has been placed in life assurance and pension funds. Borrowing by the personal sector has continued to predominantly take the form of loans for house purchase but borrowing from the banks has also grown sharply subsequent to the abolition of credit controls in the early 1980s (see below). Industrial and commercial companies' liabilities have also increased in relation to GDP but to a lesser extent. Companies have continued to rely strongly on banks for their

Diagram 7.   **Net lending by sector**
Per cent of GDP

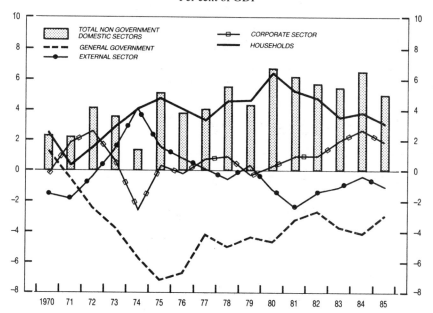

Source: *United Kingdom National Accounts,* 1986.

external funds, although most recently there has been a shift towards the capital market, in particular the new long-dated Eurosterling market (see below). Companies devote considerable resources to direct investment overseas: there was a sharp increase in their proportion of external assets after the abolition of exchange controls in 1979, which, however, has been partly reversed since then. In the 1980s, the public sector has stopped lending to the private sector; the major part of its financing needs has been provided by the sale of government securities.

A wide range of non-bank financial institutions have acted as important intermediaries in channelling funds from savers to investors. The non-financial private sector's claims on and borrowing from banks amounts only to one-sixth and one-fourth, respectively, of total assets and liabilities. This compares, e.g., with corresponding ratios of one-half and two-thirds for Germany. An outstanding feature of United Kingdom financial markets is the importance of life insurance and pension funds. The proportion of personal sector assets held with investment institutions has increased from one-fourth in the mid-1970s to about 45 per cent, compared with less than 30 per cent in the United States and less than 20 per cent in Japan and Germany[2]. In most countries the balance of deposits of the non-financial private sector has swung from banks to other financial institutions. This tendency has been particularly pronounced, however, in the United Kingdom (Table 13) where the largest part of personal sector deposits is placed with building societies (see below). Nevertheless, as noted above, total bank deposits have expanded extremely rapidly in the 1980s as the banks have obtained substantial new deposits from overseas. Although bank lending overseas has also grown explosively (Table 13), the banking sector has continued to switch funds from overseas to the domestic economy.

Table 13. Financial transactions between sectors[1]

Per cent of GDP at market prices, 1973-77 (A) and 1981-85 (B)

	Personal sector		Industrial and commercial companies		Public sector		Banking sector		Other financial institutions		Overseas sector	
	A	B	A	B	A	B	A	B	A	B	A	B
Notes and coin	0.3	0.1	0.4	–	-0.7	-0.2	–	–	–	–	–	–
Bank deposits	1.8	1.3	1.2	1.1	0.2	0.1	-4.9	-13.3	0.5	1.4	1.2	9.3
Deposits with other financial institutions	3.6	3.6	0.1	0.1	–	–	–	–	-3.7	-3.8	0.1	–
Life assurance and pension funds	4.3	5.4	–	–	–	-0.2	–	–	-4.3	-5.2	–	–
General government debt	1.6	1.6	0.2	–	-6.0	-3.4	1.0	-0.3	3.1	1.8	0.1	0.3
Company securities	–	-1.0	-0.6	-0.1	–	-0.3	-0.2	-0.3	-0.1	1.1	–	0.6
Overseas securities	-1.4	0.1	0.7	0.6	0.1	–	0.2	1.8	1.0	1.2	0.3	-3.7
Bank lending	-0.4	-1.7	-2.8	-1.2	-0.3	–	3.9	11.8	-0.3	-1.3	–	-7.7
Loans for house purchase	-3.2	-4.9	–	–	0.4	–	0.1	1.1	2.7	3.8	–	–
Public sector loans	–	–	-0.1	–	0.6	–	–	–	–	–	–	–
Other borrowing (including identified trade credit)	-0.1	-0.2	–	–	-0.2	0.2	–	–	0.2	-0.2	-0.4	–
Investment abroad	–	–	1.3	1.3	–	–	–	-0.2	0.1	–	0.1	0.1
Overseas investment in the United Kingdom	–	–	-1.5	-0.6	0.9	-0.2	0.3	–	–	–	-1.4	-1.2
Official currency financing	–	–	–	–	-0.5	-0.7	-0.1	0.1	–	–	1.5	0.7
Other (including unidentified)	-1.0	-0.9	0.4	0.4	–	–	–	–	0.1	0.2	1.2	-0.2
Financial surplus/deficit[2]	5.4	3.9	-0.9	1.8	-5.6	-3.3	0.5	0.7	-1.0	-1.2	1.5	-1.2

1. Acquisition of assets or reduction in liabilities is shown positive; sales of assets or increase in liabilities negative.
2. Residual error not included in figures for 1981-85.
Sources: Wilson Committee Report and Financial Statistics.

London as an international financial centre

As an international financial centre London ranks in the top three with New York and Tokyo. Despite the rise of new competitors, the United Kingdom has retained a leading role in the international banking markets, particularly in Eurocurrency activity. The world's largest one hundred banks are all represented in London. Banks located in the United Kingdom, both British and foreign-owned, hold just under a quarter of the international claims booked in the BIS reporting area, considerably more than the banks in Japan and the United States, respectively (Table 14). London's share of Eurobanking activity (cross-border lending in *foreign* currencies) is rather higher and its leadership is even more pronounced in the rapidly expanding Eurobond market. Some three-quarters of the secondary market turnover of Eurobonds are estimated to pass through the City. Moreover, London is still the world's leader in insurance and reinsurance. The Stock Exchange, however, no longer ranks among the largest in the world. In terms of turnover, it is in fifth position, far behind New York, Tokyo and NASDAQ (the American electronic over-the-counter system), and just behind the German exchanges (Diagram 8). In terms of market capitalisation of domestic shares, it is the third largest. An impressive number of overseas equities are also listed on the London Stock Exchange; traditionally active trading in non-United Kingdom securities has taken place mainly outside the Exchange, though this is likely to change in consequence of the regulatory structure which is in the process of being set up.

Table 14. **Shares of international bank lending**

Percentage at end-December

	1973	1975	1978	1980	1981	1982	1983	1984	1985	1986
United Kingdom	27.5	29.3	24.7	26.4	26.2	26.2	24.9	24.3	24.5	23.3
Other Europe	39.9	36.4	39.1	36.7	32.1	29.9	27.0	26.5	28.3	28.2
United States and Canada	11.6	12.5	12.5	12.3	14.0	17.4	17.2	17.7	15.0	13.3
Japan	8.1	6.2	5.5	6.2	7.1	7.2	8.2	8.9	10.4	15.0
Other centres	12.9	15.6	18.2	18.4	20.6	19.3	22.7	22.6	21.8	20.2
Memorandum item:										
United Kingdom ($ billion)	95	180	302	495	594	646	658	664	797	957

Source: Bank of England.

Without the Euromarkets, i.e. markets for deposits, loans and securities denominated in currencies held outside their country of origin, London might have lost its position as a leading financial centre. These markets, initially almost exclusively in dollars, were made possible in the late 1950s when several countries decided to make their currencies freely convertible for non-residents. Encouraged by large external deficits and the imposition of regulations in the United States in the 1960s, they were given a further boost in the 1970s by the large balances accumulated by the OPEC countries following the oil price rise. London was the favoured location for the recycling of oil funds after the two oil shocks. In the early 1980s liabilities to the oil exporters accounted for one-sixth of the total external liabilities of banks in the United Kingdom. As noted above, it was mainly the combined effect of London's historic importance and a regulatory environment sympathetic to the pursuit of international

37

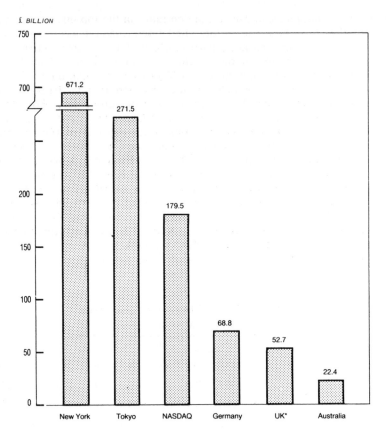

Diagram 8. **Equity turnover in major stock exchanges 1985**

£ BILLION

* Turnover has been halved for comparison purposes.
Source: The Stock Exchange, *Quality of Markets*, October 1986.

banking which made of it the largest centre of the Euromarkets; other factors include the concentration of a full range of financial services in a very small area, the standard of supporting services, and time zone advantages. In order to maintain the United Kingdom's leading position in world financial markets, the authorities have pursued a consistent policy of market liberalisation, removing remaining exchange controls (see below) and encouraging foreign banks and institutions to locate in London.

The number of foreign-owned banks (including branches and subsidiaries) in London rose from about 100 in the mid-1960s to almost 500 at the end of 1985 (Table 15), significantly exceeding the number of British-owned banks in the United Kingdom. About 120 foreign securities houses are established in the City. In 1986 the number of foreign banks seems to have more or less stabilised while employment in foreign banks and securities houses has continued to grow rapidly, reflecting partly the recruitment of new staff but mainly the acquisition of established United Kingdom firms in the context of the Big Bang in the City (see below). Employment in foreign banks and security houses is estimated to have exceeded

38

50 000 in 1986, compared with less than 10 000 twenty years ago. At present, 63 countries have direct bank representation in London. In terms of numbers of banks, the United States ranks first, while in terms of market share, Japanese banks have become the largest group (Table 15). In late 1985, almost 40 per cent of Japanese-owned banks' international business was accounted for by their London branches and subsidiaries, and the scale of international business conducted by Japanese banks in London approached that of all banks in Japan[3]. Foreign banks (including consortium banks) account for about 80 per cent of international bank lending in London, slightly more than ten years ago (Table 15). The foreign banks have also turned their attention to the United Kingdom domestic markets. They have increased their share of sterling and foreign-currency loans to British residents to more than one-fifth and about three-quarters, respectively, and taken an active part in corporate lending in the United Kingdom. The presence of foreign banks and securities firms has made a substantial contribution to both London's international position and the development of domestic financial markets. By increasing competitive pressure they are promoting efficiency and encouraging structural adjustment. However, there is a risk that domestic firms may be overwhelmed by foreign institutions, which have, in many cases, a much stronger capital base. While the authorities have not changed their policy of providing free access to domestic financial markets they are pressing for reciprocal opportunities overseas, especially in the world's leading financial centres, for British institutions. Recent legislation (see below) provides for reciprocity requirements and has increased the authorities' powers to enforce them.

Table 15. **Geographical origin and market shares of foreign banks**

	Number of banks established in London	Shares of business in London (per cent of international liabilities)		Business booked in London as a per cent of country's international liabilities
	End-1985	End-1975	End-1985	End-September 1985
United States	80	38	16	25
Japan	43	13	31	38
Germany	18			25
France	27			12
Italy	23			20
EEC	104	6	12	16
Other overseas	263	17	19	35
Total	490	79[1]	81[1]	32

1. Including consortium banks.
Source: Bank of England Quarterly Bulletin, September 1986.

Although London has remained a leading financial centre, its dominant position has been gradually eroded. As noted above, the United Kingdom's share of world exports of financial services has declined since the 1960s, though at a slower pace in recent years[4]. Its share of international bank lending has dropped from almost 30 per cent in the mid-1970s to below one-quarter, with a tendency to decrease again in recent years subsequent to some recovery in the early 1980s (Table 14). The share of other European centres fell to an even greater extent. Also, some of the fall in the United Kingdom's recorded market share reflects the expansion of the reporting area and exchange rate movements, but there seems to have been an underlying reduction of about 3 percentage points over the last decade[5]. A Constant Market Share Analysis, using a methodology applied in the analysis of merchandise export performance, carried out by the OECD for the 1978-85 period, points to a weakening in the banks' competitive position. Over this period, their international lending has shifted to markets growing more rapidly than average. Hence, the fall in the United Kingdom-based banks' world market share reflected other influences than changes in the geographical structure of demand, including possible failure to adjust to the changing structure of demand for financial products and loss in competitiveness.

Growth of overseas earnings in insurance and other brokerage has been lower than in banking. Anecdotal evidence suggests that insurance has been affected by protectionism abroad and the development of competing "Lloyd's type" insurance markets overseas. But the loss in market shares has been most pronounced in securities trading. Over the last ten years turnover on the London Stock Exchange has grown at only half the rate achieved by the New York, Tokyo and German Exchanges. As noted above, an important parallel market in Eurobonds and, more recently, international equities has developed in London. But part of the market for international and United Kingdom company shares has shifted overseas, in particular to New York where shares are traded in the form of American Depositary Receipts (ADR) at lower transaction costs (see below).

Concerned with the United Kingdom securities industry's ability to compete in domestic and international markets, the authorities have encouraged structural change, including the removal of barriers to foreign entry into an exchange that was constituted as a private club. In the context of those reforms, which culminated in the Big Bang (see below), the Stock Exchange has agreed with the International Securities Regulatory Organisation (ISRO), which represents the big foreign securities firms, to establish a single international and domestic equity market and to merge their respective regulatory functions. This should enhance London's prospects as a major centre for trading international securities. The European Community's decision to gradually remove all barriers to capital movements will present substantial opportunities for the City, given its unparalleled expertise in financial services. However, the worldwide trend towards financial market liberalisation will tend to increase the relative attraction of other centres, all the more so as prudential controls have been tightened in the United Kingdom (see below). Besides New York and Tokyo, London is the logical third leg in the world's emerging around-the-clock trading system. But the application of new information and communication technologies also weakens the case for the physical concentration of financial services. Nonetheless, the existing infrastructure together with the depth of the market and the wide range of instruments available should help to maintain London's position as a major financial centre.

Financial institutions and markets

For decades the British financial system was remarkably stable in terms of its structure and the operation of individual financial institutions. Since the early 1970s or so the pace of change has, however, accelerated markedly. The importance of non-bank financial institutions in domestic intermediation has increased significantly (Table 16 and Annex III). Traditional lines of demarcation have been eroded, as financial institutions have diversified their activities. Major changes in the 1980s include the softening of boundaries between banks and building societies, the inroads made into domestic banking markets by overseas banks, and, most recently, the erosion of the distinction between traditional and investment banks, with the acquisition of securities houses by banks in the context of the reform of securities markets.

Table 16. **Main intermediaries' shares**

As a per cent of liabilities

	1970	1980	1981	1982	1983	1984	1985
Banks[1]	32.0	29.8	30.4	28.1	26.6	26.0	25.8
Building societies	17.4	19.7	19.3	18.7	17.9	17.9	17.8
Insurance companies	26.5	25.4	25.1	26.5	26.2	26.2	25.7
Pension funds	15.5	21.0	21.4	23.2	25.4	26.1	26.7
Investment trusts	7.3	3.3	3.0	2.8	3.1	3.0	3.1
Finance houses	1.3	0.8	0.8	0.7	0.8	0.8	0.8
Total	100	100	100	100	100	100	100
£ billion	58.4	256.7	295.9	362.6	436.7	510.3	588.6
Per cent of GDP	131	129	136	154	169	185	195

1. Sterling deposits with U.K. monetary sector, including Trustee Savings Banks.
Sources: H. Rose, *Change in financial intermediation in the United Kingdom*, Oxford Review of Economic Policy, Vol. 2 (1986), No. 4 and *Financial Statistics*.

Deposit-taking institutions

The deposit-taking institutions comprise commercial banks, building societies and finance houses (Annex III). Given the trend towards financial conglomerates marketing the full range of financial services, the traditional distinction between clearing banks, merchant banks and discount houses is becoming increasingly blurred. Initially engaged in retail business, the *clearing banks* have expanded into wholesale and international banking. Despite the emergence of the Euromarkets and the arrival of a large number of foreign banks, the bulk of sterling bank deposits is still held with clearing banks while the overseas banks are mainly handling foreign currency deposits. The London and Scottish clearing banks and other regional banks maintain a considerable branch network spread throughout the United Kingdom. If, for purely stylistic reasons, the United Kingdom and London are used interchangeably throughout the text, it should be borne in mind that a significant part of domestic and even international banking business takes place outside London. Although their share of total intermediary balance sheets has continued to fall (Table 16), banks in general and clearers in particular appear to have stemmed the loss of their share of domestic deposit markets, becoming active lenders to the personal sector, in direct competition with the building societies. Having been already involved in merchant banking (through subsidiaries) and the marketing of securities (through unit trusts), clearing banks have set up large new security trading operations in the context of the Big Bang (see below). There has been a tendency for *savings banks* to be gradually integrated in the banking sector. The reorganisation of the Trustee Savings Banks (TSB), which started in the 1970s, was brought to an end by the TSB flotation in October 1986. Other institutions have been allowed to provide a wider range of banking services.

The *building society sector* has been one of the major growth elements in the financial system, more than doubling its share in the sterling deposit market since the 1960s. Building societies' sterling liabilities to the public are greater than those of the clearing banks and, in terms of deposits from the personal sector, larger than the total for all banks. More than half of personal sector liquid assets is held with building societies. Among other things, their extraordinary expansion reflects the favourable tax treatment to loans for house purchase and other tax advantages (see below). Raising funds predominently in the retail saving market, the societies have increasingly entered the wholesale money market as borrowers, as they have to face increased competition by banks. Recent legislation (see below) has allowed them to increase their banking activities but still limits their proportion of wholesale funding. While the clearing banks have reduced their branch network, that of the building societies has grown sharply. At the same time, however, there has been a pronounced concentration process. Indeed, since the early 1970s, the number of societies has fallen from about 400 to about 150.

Other financial institutions

Other financial institutions comprise life and general insurance companies, pension funds, unit trusts and investment trust companies. These institutions are more important than generally elsewhere, providing about one-half of domestic intermediation (Table 16 and Annex III) and collectively dominating the securities markets. The assets of self-administered pension funds have shown the most rapid expansion (Diagram 9). At about 4 per cent, the ratio of life assurance premiums to GDP is among the highest in the OECD area. Given substantial tax advantages, life assurance and pension funds (LAPFs) have become major vehicles for personal sector saving. More recently, about two-thirds of personal sector savings have been channelled into LAPFs. They hold about one-half of British government stocks and over one-half of the total ordinary share issue of United Kingdom companies quoted on the London Stock Exchange. The most significant change in LAPF portfolios has been the marked rise in the share of overseas assets since the abolition of exchange controls in 1979. General (non-life) insurance represents only a small part of domestic insurance business but is the largest foreign exchange earner among the financial institutions (see above) due mainly to the leading position of Lloyd's in international insurance markets. Foreign business accounts for almost 40 per cent of total general insurance business. After losing ground until the early 1980s, partly due to tax disadvantages, investment and unit trusts have strongly expanded in recent years.

Securities markets

The Stock Exchange is the central market in public sector and United Kingdom company securities. Equities' share in turnover has markedly risen in recent years (to over one-quarter) but the gilt-edged (government bond) market still represents the major segment. Corporate bonds are negligible. The Unlisted Securities Market (see below) has remained relatively small. Shares of small United Kingdom companies are mainly traded in the over-the-counter market, which has most recently been complemented by the Third Market (see below). As noted above, Eurobonds are traded for the most part outside organised capital markets, and the more recent emergence of an off-exchange market in international equities in London has involved trading not only in foreign equities but also in major United Kingdom stocks in both registered and ADR form. Another important market, which has developed outside the Stock Exchange, is the London International Financial Futures Exchange (LIFFE) which trades financial futures and options. These are also traded on the Stock Exchange together with options on many individual stocks. Before last year's structural reforms the Stock Exchange was organised in terms of a strict separation of capacity between broking firms and dealers (jobbers). Single capacity, ownership rules (preventing foreigners and British merchant and clearing banks from becoming members) and minimum commission arrangements constrained the Exchange's ability to adapt and to compete. Those restrictions were gradually eased from 1984 (see below) and completely abolished in late 1986 (the Big Bang). At the same time, the gilt market was opened to outsiders and a computerised quotation and information system (SEAQ) was introduced. A parallel development was the merger with ISRO (see above). Those developments should encourage off-market trading to be conducted through the renamed International Stock Exchange of the United Kingdom and the Republic of Ireland.

Diagram 9. Total assets of the major financial institutions

£ billion

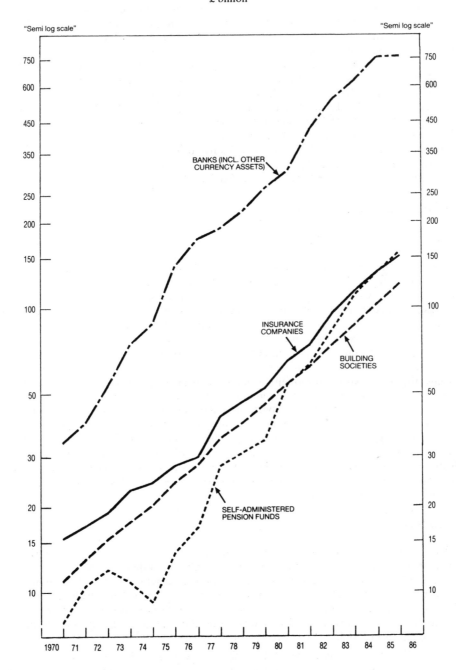

"Semi log scale"

"Semi log scale"

BANKS (INCL. OTHER CURRENCY ASSETS)

INSURANCE COMPANIES

BUILDING SOCIETIES

SELF-ADMINISTERED PENSION FUNDS

Source: *Financial Statistics.*

Money markets

The entry of overseas banks in connection with the emergence of Euromarkets has led to the development of an extensive market for wholesale funds in London, covering transactions in negotiable instruments and short-term deposits. The discount houses play a prominent role in the traditional secured money market. Acting as market-makers in the call money market and in the Treasury and commercial bill markets, they have privileged access to the Bank as lender of last resort. The role of the discount market has been reduced by the development of parallel markets, mainly in inter-bank unsecured deposits but increasingly also in certificates of deposit, since the 1960s. While banks are the main participants in the strongly expanding Eurocurrency markets, sterling market participants include also other financial institutions, local authorities, and companies. A recent innovation has been the introduction of sterling commercial paper: since April 1986 companies listed on the Stock Exchange are allowed to issue unsecured promissory notes; before they were only able to sell commercial paper in the well-developed United States' markets or Euromarkets.

The Government's financial reforms

Liberalisation measures at the turn of the 1970s

The introduction of Competition and Credit Control in the early 1970s (abolition of direct credit controls, dismantling of the clearing banks' interest rate cartel) represented an important move towards financial market liberalisation, which was, however, partly reversed by the periodic reimposition of quantitative controls through the Supplementary Special Deposits Scheme ("the corset"). Another wave of deregulation started soon after the present Government took office in 1979. Reflecting a shift in policy orientation, but also in view of the development of indigenous oil resources, official restrictions on overseas investment were relaxed, and later in the year foreign exchange controls were abolished altogether (restrictions did not extend to foreign currency business, which had allowed the development of London's Eurocurrency markets). As a consequence, the "corset", already weakened by domestic avoidance, became largely ineffective and was, therefore, abandoned in June 1980. To give markets greater influence in the process of interest rate determination, new monetary control arrangements were introduced in 1981: the continuous posting of an official minimum lending rate was abandoned and the reserve asset ratio for clearing banks replaced by a uniform requirement on all deposit-taking institutions to hold a percentage of their eligible liabilities with the Bank. Finally, official regulation of consumer instalment credit was removed in July 1982.

Recent reforms

The extensive reforms taking place in securities markets and in the regulation of the financial services industry represent a mixture of further liberalisation and greater regulation. The Big Bang on the Stock Exchange removed barriers between specialised functions and institutions. To some extent, this is also true for new legislation dealing with building societies. On the other hand, the Financial Services Act extends the scope of formal regulation and, together with the Building Societies Act and the updating of the Banking Act, tightens supervision to improve investor protection.

i) The *Big Bang* on the Stock Exchange resulted from the Government's decision, in July 1983, to exempt the Stock Exchange from the Restrictive Trade Practices Act subject to specific reforms to its rules and trading arrangements by the end of

1986. Minor changes in the commission structure and the trading rules were already made in in 1984. New ownership rules became effective in March 1986, allowing outsiders to acquire majority participation in Stock Exchange member firms and (domestic and foreign) corporate membership. On 27th October the last and major part of the reform package was brought into effect: minimum commission rates and the compulsory distinction between stockbrokers and jobbers were abandoned, and a new structure of the gilt-edged market, jointly developed by the Stock Exchange and the Bank of England, took effect (with similar rules for broker-dealers and a considerably increased number of market makers).

ii) The *Financial Services Act* 1986 represents the most comprehensive overhaul of legislation regulating investment business for over 40 years. It extends the scope of direct supervision to financial (and commodities) futures and options and to international securities. Most of the powers to authorise and regulate investment business are to be delegated to the Securities and Investments Board (SIB), a private sector body, which in turn may delegate some of them to Self Regulating Organisations (SROs). Among the SROs seeking recognition, The Securities Association (TSA) is the most important. It is the product of the merger of the Stock Exchange and the International Securities Regulatory Organisation (ISRO) and provides regulatory cover for firms conducting business in domestic and international securities. A candidate for SIB recognition as a Recognised Investment Exchange (RIE), a concept established by the Act, is, among others, the new International Stock Exchange. The Bank of England will continue to supervise the traditional lending and deposit-taking activities of banks and will have special responsibility for (sterling and foreign exchange) wholesale money markets and the gilt-edged market. Some provisions of the Financial Services Act (such as those concerning alleged insider dealing, listing requirements and, most recently, reciprocity) have already been brought into force. After the recognition of regulatory bodies (probably in the latter part of 1987) it will become a criminal offence to carry on investment business in the United Kingdom without authorisation.

iii) The *Building Societies Act* 1986, most of which became effective at the beginning of 1987, allows building societies, within a limited part of their commercial assets, to undertake some forms of lending new to them: they are now able to make unsecured loans, run insurance broking and provide a number of other financial services, including full current account facilities. Prudential supervision has been strengthened and vested in a new Building Societies Commission.

iv) The *Banking Act* 1987, which will come into force for most purposes in October 1987, will replace the 1979 Banking Act. A Board of Banking Supervision will be responsible for advising the Bank of England on the exercise of its supervisory function. The existing two-tier system of authorisation and supervision is to be abolished and replaced by a single set of criteria applicable to all institutions. The Bank of England is to be given powers to obtain information from banks and connected parties and to object to proposed and existing shareholder control of United Kingdom incorporated banks on prudential grounds. The Act also includes powers to enable the authorities to object to proposed shareholder control from countries which do not treat United Kingdom persons on equal basis with regard to banking, insurance and financial business.

The financial system and economic performance

As demonstrated above, the financial sector is among the most dynamic of the economy and has maintained an importance in world financial markets which far exceeds that of the country's economic base. Also, the financial system would appear to be performing well its intermediation role between deficit and surplus units. Nevertheless, there are some problem areas, although they may be less important than generally elsewhere. One source of distortion is the taxation system which privileges certain forms of savings. This affects competition between different types of financial institutions and may distort the allocation of savings between competing investment uses. Market segmentation due to legal and customary barriers — within the domestic market as well as between the international and domestic market — has declined as a result of tax changes and financial reforms. Liberalisation measures have increased competitive pressure and cost efficiency but complicated the task of monetary policy and prudential supervision.

Operation and internal efficiency of the system

One way of assessing the efficiency of intermediation is to compare relevant cost and profit ratios drawn from balance sheet statistics. Available indicators for the London clearing banks, which account for less than one-third of the monetary sector, suggest that the cost of intermediation is relatively high by international comparison (Diagram 10). As differences in accounting conventions and the importance of off-balance sheet business limit the comparability of ratio levels across countries, more emphasis should be put on their development over time. The ratio of operating expenses to total assets fell in the first half of the 1980s, indicating efficiency gains. This allowed some recovery in the net income/asset ratio, though apparently not yet back to levels prevailing in the late 1970s. Nevertheless, the gross earnings margin, an indicator for the overall cost of intermediation, has shown a trend decline since the latter part of the 1970s while being stable or rising in most other countries. Net income from other sources than interest is higher and has grown more than generally elsewhere. Its share in gross earnings increased from one-third at the turn of the 1970s to two-thirds in the mid-1980s (Table 17). Net interest margins have dropped markedly in the 1980s and appear now to be close to levels prevailing in other larger Member countries. Their decline has largely reflected developments in domestic markets. Interest margins on international business have remained broadly stable, though at a considerably lower level, reflecting the large interbank component of foreign loans. To some extent, the observed narrowing in interest margins may be attributable to the decline in interest rate levels. The presence of non-interest bearing deposits normally implies a less than one-for-one change in the average cost of funds in response to a change in the level of interest rates (endowment income effect). Interest margins have also been squeezed by the falling proportion of non-interest bearing deposits resulting from increasing competition between banks and building societies. Interest spreads, which do not reflect these influences, have not shown the clear underlying decline of margins. Increased competition has probably contributed to the marked fall in capital ratios during the first half of the 1980s (Table 17), which appears to have been reversed, however, more recently, as bank profitability has improved.

Corresponding indicators for the building societies sector, which is of equal importance in domestic intermediation, are generally much lower (Table 18). Building societies can operate on a considerably finer margin between borrowing and lending rates than other institutions providing retail financial services because of their mutual status with no requirement to pay out a dividend, a low reserve requirement reflecting their asset composition, and low management expenses due to a relatively simple operation. The

46

Diagram 10. **Cost efficiency and profitability in the banking sector**

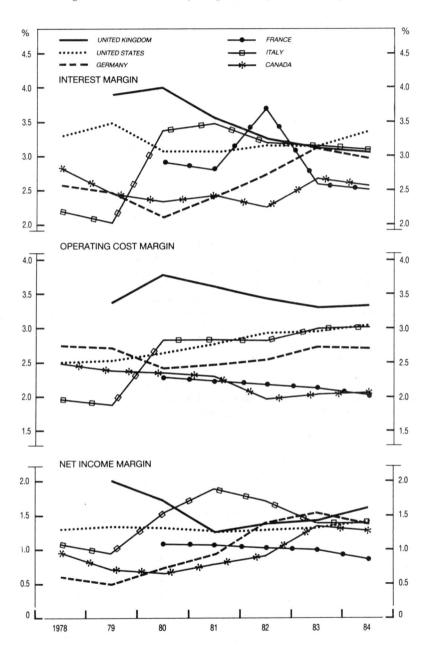

Source: *Bank profitability*, OECD, Paris, 1987.

Table 17. **London clearing banks: financial indicators**

As a per cent of average total assets

	1980	1981	1982	1983	1984
Net interest income	4.00	3.56	3.25	3.11	3.06
Non-interest income	1.48	1.28	1.54	1.61	1.85
Gross income	5.49	4.84	4.79	4.71	4.92
Operating expenses	3.77	3.59	3.42	3.29	3.32
Net income	1.72	1.25	1.37	1.42	1.60
Capital and reserves[1]	5.66	4.80	4.57	4.66	3.62
Memorandum item:					
Staff (thousand)	272	277	281	283	287

1. As a per cent of end-year total assets.
Source: Bank profitability, OECD. Paris, 1987.

societies' ratio of operating expenses to total assets rose markedly until the early 1980s, albeit from a very low level, but has stabilised in recent years, mirroring the decelerating growth of branch networks (Table 18). Other income has been of minor importance and relatively stable. Interest margins have tended to rise in spite of increased competitive pressure, given higher operating costs due to non-price competition, as well as higher reserve requirements and tax payments (see below). Into the 1980s, the building societies maintained an interest rate cartel which, if anything, tended to keep lending costs down. This price policy implied a transfer of income from depositors to borrowers, mostly mortgage holders. Facing increased competition by banks in the mortgage market but also on the borrowing side, the societies have adopted a more commercial approach to their business, setting interest rates more in line with market conditions.

Since the erosion of the interest cartel and entry of clearing banks, margins are clearly determined competitively in mortgage markets. But the higher degree of concentration and cost of entry in retail banking, along with the low interest elasticity of consumer demand, appear to have protected margins in non-mortgage lending to the personal sector, notwithstanding some signs of a narrowing. Wide differences in some non-mortgage personal

Table 18. **Building societies: financial indicators**

As a per cent of average total assets

	1978	1980	1981	1982	1983	1984	1985
Net interest income	1.19	1.53	1.72	1.51	1.32	1.45	1.92
Non-interest income	0.20	0.23	0.26	0.25	0.31	0.32	0.28
Gross earnings[1]	1.40	1.76	1.98	1.76	1.63	1.76	2.19
Operating expenses	0.80	1.17	1.26	1.27	1.26	1.18	1.13
Net earnings[1]	0.59	0.60	0.72	0.49	0.37	0.58	1.07
Pre-tax profits	0.96	0.72	0.94	0.95	1.01	0.91	1.15
Capital and reserves[2]	3.47	3.51	3.67	3.76	2.93	4.00	4.07
Memorandum items:							
Number of institutions	316	273	253	227	206	190	167
Number of branches	4595	5684	6162	6480	6643	6816	6927
Staff (thousand)	44.9	52.7	55.3	58.1	61.2	63.1	65.7

1. Excluding investment profits.
2. As a per cent of end-year total assets.
Source: Building Societies Association.

loan interest rates seem to persist, although these may in part reflect differences in non-price conditions. There is evidence that margins in corporate lending have narrowed over the past decade[6]. The complexity of lending terms, along with the absence of published information, probably restricts competition, but corporate borrowers have access to a variety of lenders, including overseas banks (accounting already for about 40 per cent of bank lending to the business sector, see below).

The tax system has been made more neutral as between different financial institutions, instruments and channels. In particular, reflecting the 1984 Budget, the income and corporation tax treatment of banks and building societies has been brought closer into line, life insurance premium relief has been withdrawn from new contracts, capital gains tax exemption of government securities has been extended to holdings of certain company bonds, and the income tax surcharge on investment income has been abolished. Moreover, the staged reduction in the rate of corporation tax has made companies' choice between equity and debt finance less influenced by tax considerations. But some distortions remain. Complete neutrality of treatment for different types of financial institutions and assets is not necessarily desirable given the different social and economic objectives to which they contribute. But, in particular, it has been suggested that there is little logic underlying the tax treatment of savings in the United Kingdom[7]. However, while each fiscal incentive for saving on investment has its origin in a conscious policy decision, it is the sum of these incentives which may not look particularly logical in relation to savings and investment as a whole. Discrimination between different forms of saving has been accompanied by enormous changes in the composition of personal net worth over the last quarter century. The proportion of privileged assets such as dwellings (with mortgage), pension funds and insurance contracts (no longer privileged) has increased from less than one-half to more than two-thirds, with only a negligible part of the total savings flow over that period going into other types of assets. The result has been a significant increase in the amount of investment channelled through institutions. Institutional investors appear to have a strong preference for shares of low specific risk. By encouraging flows into such institutions, the tax system may be leading to higher risk premiums throughout the market than would otherwise be the case. Differences in fiscal privilege are such that changes in the underlying real rate of return on different assets would not be able to equalise the post-tax returns. The influence of tax considerations on investment decisions is unlikely to improve the efficiency of capital markets.

Until last year domestic securities markets were characterised by relatively high transaction costs and inadequately capitalised firms. The rapid expansion of international portfolios of United Kingdom institutions since the abolition of exchange controls benefited Stock Exchange members scarcely at all and, as noted, the market in leading United Kingdom equities was shifting away from the Exchange. The Big Bang of last October more than doubled the number of equity market makers and led to a sharp increase in turnover and a substantial fall in transaction costs, as extra competition and liquidity put downward pressure on (freed) commission rates and market spreads[8]. Equity turnover doubled in the six months to March. Part of the fall in transaction costs resulted from a reduction in the rate of stamp duty from 1 per cent to $\frac{1}{2}$ per cent as from October (following an earlier reduction from 2 per cent). Commission rates for large equity deals have dropped from about 0.4 per cent to about 0.2 per cent; for very large deals they are now even lower, and many institutional investors deal directly with firms on a net-of-commission basis. Commissions paid on small transactions by individual investors, on the other hand, have dropped only marginally to slightly above $1\frac{1}{2}$ percent. Competition has increased even more in the restructured gilt-edged market where turnover grew sixfold in the six months to March. About one-half of business is done, however, between market-makers whose number has sharply increased. Commission rates in this market have dropped to 0.1 per cent for individual investors and below that level for institutions so that many dealers cannot cover their costs and may have to pull out of the market. So far, however, much higher turnover since the Big Bang has limited trading losses and there has been only one withdrawal from market-making in equities.

Allocative efficiency of the system

a) *Patterns of business finance*

There is broad agreement that, in general, conditions for business finance are satisfactory and raising of capital has not been a constraint on real investment. Investment performance, as measured by the ratio to GDP, is not out of line with that of most other Member countries. The January 1985 Survey concluded that the main problem for the United Kingdom is unlikely to stem from an insufficient quantity of investment but rather from the inefficient use or poor quality of investment. There are, however, indications that the situation may have changed more recently, latest estimates for capital productivity showing an improved performance both compared with past experience and that of most other countries. The major financial constraint on real investment identified by the Wilson Report[9], namely the price of finance in relation to expected profitability, would seem to continue to play a role, however. Real interest rates to corporate borrowers have remained at high levels, also by international comparison. In contrast, the real rate of return of non-North Sea oil companies, though recovering in recent years, is low by international standards. Hence, the cost of capital appears to have continued to exceed the average rate of return on companies' fixed assets. It is true that evidence of the sensitivity of investment to the cost of finance is by no means conclusive, and enterprises have relied to a considerable (and growing) extent on internal resources (Diagram 11). But the high cost of capital relative to company profitability may help to explain the fact that, atypically, the corporate sector (even exclunding North Sea oil) has been a net lender (Table 12), investing to a considerable extent in financial assets rather than in physical capital (Diagram 11). Another possibly worrying feature is that, in relation to investment, expenditure on mergers and acquisitions has grown sharply (to about one-quarter in 1984-85 and about one-half in 1986, approaching the levels reached in previous merger booms). This has been seen, in part, as a manifestation of "short-termism" due to the fact that about 70 per cent of equity in the United Kingdom is owned by financial institutions and funds who are alleged to be interested in short-term performance rather than providing support for long-term projects.

The United Kingdom financial system is broadly market-based, with highly active securities markets, dominated by institutional investors, providing a major source of finance for industrial and commercial companies. This is evidenced by the structure of corporate liabilities, as measured by the debt/equity ratio. At a similar level as in the United States, the latter is considerably lower than in countries where banks play the dominating role in the intermediation process, such as Germany and Japan. It has decreased in the 1980s, as generally elsewhere, influenced by rising equity prices and improving profitability (Table 19). Differences between market-based and bank-based systems have tended to decline, however, due to institutional changes and the trends of globalisation of capital markets and securitisation of bank lending. Consequently, the pattern of the flows of funds to firms has been converging (Table 20). Notwithstanding a trend reversal more recently, the recourse of United Kingdom companies to external equity finance and fixed-rate long-term bond finance was relatively small since the 1970s while the role of banks increased. Encouraged, among other things, by increasing competition in domestic markets from foreign banks, who had originally come to London primarily to develop their international lending interests, British

Diagram 11. **Uses and sources of funds of industrial and commercial companies**

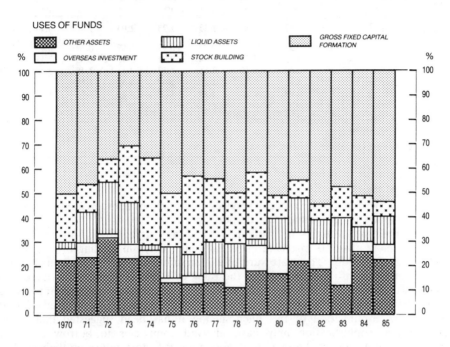

USES OF FUNDS

OTHER ASSETS LIQUID ASSETS GROSS FIXED CAPITAL FORMATION

OVERSEAS INVESTMENT STOCK BUILDING

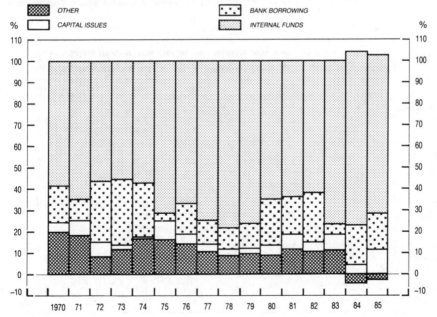

SOURCES OF FUNDS

OTHER BANK BORROWING

CAPITAL ISSUES INTERNAL FUNDS

Source: Financial Statistics.

Table 19. **Debt/equity ratios of the non-financial corporate sector[1]**

	1966-73	1974-79	1980	1981	1982	1983	1984	1985
United Kingdom	0.67	1.38	1.13	1.23	1.03	1.87	0.74	0.70[2]
United States	0.54	0.96	0.77	0.92	0.87	0.78	0.90	0.83
Japan	3.08	3.31	3.14	2.91	2.92	2.68	2.11	1.82[2]
Germany[3]	2.38	3.36	3.85	4.13	4.11	3.48	3.42	2.39
France	1.17[4]	1.33	1.23	1.40	1.55	1.56	..	..
Canada	0.99	1.22	1.14	1.27	1.34	1.14	1.12	1.08[2]

1. Gross liabilities excluding equity and trade credit as a proportion of equity at market prices, except for France and Canada where equity is at book values.
2. Estimated.
3. All enterprises excluding housing.
4. 1970-73.
Sources: National balance-sheet data and *OECD Financial Statistics*.

banks started to provide a wider range of services, and relations between industry and finance have become much closer in the past decade or so.

Despite the improvement in profitability and an aggregate self-financing ratio of investment of more than 100 per cent in recent years, external funding of companies has continued to grow rapidly. There are various explanations for the simultaneous build-up of debt and financial assets. Research within the Bank of England suggests that increments in profits are primarily used, in the short run, to build up liquid assets rather than to run down stocks of debt, while higher investment, again in the short run, is largely financed out of debt. To explain the continuation of this phenomenon it has been suggested that increased competition and sophistication may have allowed companies to borrow at relatively favourable conditions and at the same time obtain a satisfactory return on their holdings of liquid assets. To a large extent, however, growth in liquid financial assets can be associated

Table 20. **Issue of shares and securities by private non-financial enterprises**

Percentage of gross fixed capital formation of the private non-residential sector

	1979	1980	1981	1982	1983	1984	1985
United Kingdom							
Shares	4.2	3.8	6.9	3.8	6.7	3.7	9.0
Securities	4.4	4.6	7.8	4.5	7.9	4.6	11.3
United States							
Shares	3.6	6.1	5.7	6.5	10.3	3.1	4.2
Securities	9.3	14.3	11.8	11.6	14.8	14.2	20.3
Japan							
Shares	4.2	3.8	5.3	5.0	3.3	4.0	3.1
Securities	8.1	5.9	8.7	8.7	7.1	9.0	9.0
Germany							
Shares	2.6	3.2	2.0	2.6	3.4	2.4	3.8
Securities	1.0	3.6	2.4	4.3	3.4	3.2	6.3
France							
Shares	3.9	4.2	7.0	6.6	9.4	9.6	12.5
Securities	7.3	6.9	8.6	10.9	13.7	13.8	16.8

Sources: *OECD Financial Statistics* and *OECD National Accounts*.

with a continued wave of mergers and acquisitions, although the latter has been increasingly undertaken by means of capital issues. Companies' relatively high bank borrowing (Diagram 11) led to a gradual rise in capital gearing (net financial debt as a proportion of total trading assets) during the first half of the 1980s. Income gearing (net interest payments as a proportion of profits after tax) has also tended to rise slightly more recently, following a sharp drop from the high levels in the early 1980s (resulting from high interest rates and depressed profits in the recession). Both ratios have continued to be low, though, by international comparison. But there are substantial sectoral differences, and the interest burden is markedly higher for small business for which banks continue to be the prime source of funds.

Bank lending to business has sharply declined most recently (Diagram 11). One factor contributing was the deceleration of leasing as a result of reduced tax advantages. But, as shown in Table 20, issues of shares and securities by private non-financial enterprises have tended to rise in relation to investment in the last few years, though from a very low level. The long-term corporate bond market has failed to recover, however, in spite of the encouragement provided by the above-mentioned tax measures. The new sterling commercial paper market has shown a steady but not spectacular level of activity, given the remaining restrictions (see above) and strong competition from the corresponding Euromarket. Share issues, however, have continued to rise sharply, though in part due to special factors (such as the sizeable British Gas flotation).

b) *Moves to increase equity participation*

Although United Kingdom companies have generally operated with a wider equity base and lower capital gearing than companies in many other countries, the deterioration in the balance sheet structure of the corporate sector in the 1970s and into the 1980s (Table 19) had been a matter of concern. In order to strengthen the equity base of companies, it was essential to restore profitability, as internally generated funds have typically provided the bulk of their finance, but also to supplement internal funds by improved access to external equity capital. During its term of office, the Government has taken a wide range of measures to encourage equity finance and equity participation of individuals in particular. "Wider share ownership" is expected to contribute to the emergence of a new "enterprise culture" with increased contacts between individuals and companies and a better understanding of how business works. Institutional investors, despite their position as major shareholders of United Kingdom companies, have maintained little direct contact with the companies in which they invested and have been reluctant to take new risks, which can make it more difficult for small and new firms to raise funds. Hence, the trend towards concentrating share ownership with financial institutions is believed to make the market less effective as a source of investment capital.

The supply of equity finance for small and new companies has been significantly improved by the development of venture capital funds and junior stock markets. *Venture capital funds* have expanded rapidly in the 1980s, helped by government schemes providing tax incentives for personal equity investment (see below). Their number has increased from fewer than 20 in 1979 to more than 110, and the amount invested in recent years is, as a proportion of GDP, comparable to that of the United States, accounting for two-thirds of total venture capital investment in the European Community area. The proportion of funds for start-up companies is relatively small, however, with finance for expansion on the one hand and by management buy-outs and buy-ins on the other each accounting for about one-half of the rest. The bulk of venture capital is provided by pension funds. Originally part of larger firms, such as banks, venture firms have been increasingly established as independent firms, though frequently backed by big institutions.

Since its inception in November 1980, the *Unlisted Securities Market* (USM), the first in Europe, has successfully fulfilled the role of an organised equity market for small and medium-sized companies operating in growth sectors, improving access to equity capital for these companies and reducing the cost to the company of raising funds. Conditions of admission to the USM are easier than those prevailing on the principal exchange but investor protection rules are similar. Starting with 11 companies, the USM has grown to more than 370 company quotations capitalised at almost £5 billion. Market liquidity and price volatility continues to be a problem, but the USM has become broader-based after the near-collapse of its largest sectors (oil and electronics) and has continued to expand after the Big Bang, although there were fears that securities houses, in an increasingly competitive City, would by-pass the more modest business generated by the small companies quoted on the USM. The USM could suffer, however, in the long run, from the creation of the so-called *Third Market* in January 1987. Entry requirements to the latter are less onerous, with most of the responsibilities falling to a sponsor (which has to be a Stock Exchange member), and personal investors qualify for income tax relief under the Business Expansion Scheme (see below), not available for shares quoted on the USM or the main exchange. On the other hand, the Third Market provides investors with a better regulated and more transparent environment than the over-the-counter market for shares of unquoted companies. Trading on the new market has slumped after a buoyant start, but a similar pattern was observed after the introduction of the USM in 1980.

The *Business Expansion Scheme* (BES) was set up in 1983 (as a successor to the Business Start-up Scheme) and provides generous income tax relief for new equity investment (direct or through an approved investment fund) by individuals not closely connected with the firms concerned, which must be unquoted United Kingdom companies (or companies quoted on the new Third Market). Eligibility requirements were tightened in 1986 to prevent the promotion of very sound assets (such as land and buildings). Since January, up to a certain limit, investments in ordinary shares of United Kingdom companies listed on the Stock Exchange and in unit trusts are free of tax on dividends and capital gains if they are kept in a *Personal Equity Plan* (PEP) for two years. So far interest of the public has been relatively limited. The scheme is in principle aimed at the small saver and first-time share-buyer who are unlikely to be liable for capital gains tax. Employees can acquire shares of the companies in which they work under a more lenient tax regime. The number of such *employee share schemes* has risen from 30 in 1979 to about 1 200, covering 1 ½ million employees, as tax incentives to encourage firms to introduce share ownership schemes for all their employees have been further improved. There are also tax incentives for share schemes for key employees and for savings-related share option schemes.

Besides the growth of employee share schemes it has been above all the Government's privatisation programme which has boosted wider share ownership. Most companies have been privatised by stock market flotation with special arrangements being made to encourage both employees and small investors to buy shares. The latest survey evidence suggests the number of shareholders in the United Kingdom has risen from 3 million in 1979 to 8½ million, or just under 20 per cent of the adult population, largely as a result of the British Telecom, Trustee Savings Banks and British Gas flotations since late 1984 which attracted altogether almost 10 million shareholders (of whom about 8 million are estimated to have remained on the register). Despite the privatisation programme and rising equity prices, the proportion of shares in personal sector gross wealth has risen only slightly, after falling from one-quarter in the early 1970s to one-tenth in the early 1980s. Moreover, notwithstanding greatly improved tax incentives and the removal of tax privileges for life assurance (not for pension funds), the proportion of United Kingdom equity held directly by individuals has continued to decline and is now down to about one-quarter (from more than one-half in the

1960s). The greater fall in transaction costs for large institutional investors after the Big Bang (see above) has boosted institutional trading. The latest survey also suggests that a large proportion of shareholders have a stake in only one or two companies and that share ownership is concentrated in the higher age and income groups. Hence, there is still much scope for both deepening and widening share ownership.

Impact on policies and macro-performance

a) Effectiveness of monetary policy

Containment of broad money within gradually declining target limits was the centrepiece of the Government's Medium Term Financial Strategy as unveiled in the 1980 Budget. In the event, economic policy has been more successful in achieving ultimate objectives than in meeting intermediate broad monetary targets. In view of their persistent overshooting, these have been periodically redefined, revised upwards, or even suspended (see Monetary Policy section in Part II). The re-emergence of positive real interest rates seems to have contributed to faster growth of broad money, making holding of financial assets more attractive. However, a major factor behind the breakdown of stable relationships between most monetary aggregates and nominal income appears to have been the fast pace of financial innovation and liberalisation in recent years. The removal of controls around 1980 has not only led to a surge in banking intermediation but triggered an entirely new dynamic in competition between financial intermediaries. With the entry of banks into the mortgage market, rationing of mortgage lending by building societies came to an end. To support additional lending, both banks and building societies had to offer better terms for deposits, which has led to a strong rise in the proportion of interest-bearing sight deposits. In one way or the other, these changes have tended to increase the volume of intermediation and distort the growth of interest-bearing monetary aggregates, making the trend of their income velocity less predictable.

For the personal sector, the observed simultaneous build-up of debt and liquidity can be largely explained by households rearranging their portfolio of liabilities and assets in response to the freer availability of credit, particularly at low cost and long term[10]. For companies and non-bank financial institutions, which have particularly contributed to accelerated growth of broad money, as noted above, one possible explanation for the rapid expansion of both sides of their balance sheet is that the narrowing of the costs of intermediation, i.e. the effective spread between deposit and lending rates, due to increased competition and technological change has reduced the incentive to economise on both borrowing and holding deposits. There is evidence that the demand for deposits and loans has become more elastically responsive to shifts in interest spreads while the growth of broad money and private sector bank lending has become insensitive to variations in the general level of interest rates[11]. With dividing lines between the functions carried out by the various financial intermediaries becoming blurred, minor changes in relative interest rates may lead asset holders to rearrange their portfolios. Hence, the relationship of such asset holdings to nominal income and to the general level of interest rates tends to become looser and the growth of monetary aggregates tends to become less reliable as a guide to future trends in inflation and nominal incomes.

The deregulation and structural change of financial markets has altered the ways in which the authorities are able to influence the growth of the monetary aggregates, especially broad money. In particular, the abolition of exchange controls and the liberalisation and growing integration of financial markets reduced the efficiency of the Supplementary Special Deposit Scheme (the "corset"). This was abandoned, as noted above, partly for this reason but also because of the Government's opposition to controls. Overfunding of the PSBR provided a means of influencing the growth of broad money, but it too was discontinued because of the distortionary effects it was having on financial markets. Short-term interest rates now have to carry the whole thrust of monetary policy and they may therefore be higher than if direct controls and overfunding were in operation.

b) *Problems of prudential supervision*

The described process of deregulation, innovation and structural change has also made the task of prudential supervision more demanding but at the same time also more important. The growing diversity of business of individual institutions initially exposes them to greater risks and makes it more difficult to assess their soundness. With the external separation of broking and dealing functions abolished, the risk of misconduct has increased. Hence, to improve investor protection and deal effectively with fraud, the whole framework of financial market supervision is being up-dated and extended (see above). The new system can be characterised as controlled statute-based self-regulation. However, in the wake of various financial scandals, the balance is shifting towards more statutory control: the authorities have seen to it that self-regulatory standards become more stringent (e.g. in the case of Lloyd's and the Takeover Panel) but warned that they would impose statutory controls where necessary. The new regulatory structure is expected to avoid the rigidity and higher costs of more centralised systems. It may, however, prove to be unnecessarily complex. Constructed on functional rather than institutional lines, it may pose formidable co-ordination problems between the different supervisory agencies relevant for any single financial institution conducting a wide range of business. Experience of other countries suggests, however, that there is little alternative: institution-based supervision tends to become ineffective and inconsistent when the distinction of activities becomes blurred.

Recent legislation (see above) gives the Bank of England stronger statutory powers, in particular in the prudential control of bank takeovers and large exposures. According to a recent survey, most banks were basing their capital allocation system on the minimum regulatory requirements of the central bank and, hence, had not allocated capital for all off-balance sheet items, including the full range of innovative financial instruments developed in recents years. These items will be included in a common measure of capital adequacy on which United States and United Kingdom regulators have reached agreement. Apart from these and other modifications, the new measure corresponds to the risk asset ratio calculated by the Bank for a number of years. International co-operation in the supervision and regulation of financial markets, including securities markets, is an area where urgent progress is needed, as divergent prudential standards as between different centres threaten the effectiveness of supervision in all centres.

IV. OUTLOOK AND LONG-TERM PERFORMANCE

Short-term prospects

The latest OECD forecast published in mid-June puts the OECD area annual rate of GDP growth at around $2\frac{1}{2}$ per cent over the next eighteen months or so. The United Kingdom's export markets are expected to expand fairly steadily at about $4\frac{1}{2}$ per cent, somewhat faster than world trade. The recent appreciation of sterling has partly reversed the marked improvement in competitiveness since mid-1985 but on the technical assumption of no further nominal exchange rate changes as from the 21st April, the information cut-off day for the OECD *Economic Outlook*, the effective exchange rate of sterling will remain significantly below its 1986 average. Even so, the competitive position is foreseen to deteriorate as unit labour costs are likely to increase faster than on average in trading partner countries. Hence, export market gains arising from the earlier depreciation of sterling will become smaller and are projected to be reversed. Domestically, a broadly neutral stance of fiscal policy and some tightening of monetary policy is assumed in the period ahead, with interest rates edging up in line with international developments. This policy configuration would seem to be consistent with both a constant exchange rate and gradual deceleration in monetary growth.

Domestic demand growth should remain strong this year followed by a likely slowdown in 1988 (Table 21). After a period of weak capital spending but improved profit and output expectations, intention surveys point to a marked pick-up of business investment activity in 1987. However, given the projected deterioration in international competitiveness, the upswing may peter out towards the end of next year. Stockbuilding is expected to accelerate temporarily after the sharp drop in the stock/output ratio last year. Residential construction, which rose steeply during 1986, is likely to grow at a slower pace. Budget plans point to declining public investment and slower growth of public consumption, following the relatively rapid expansion in 1986. Private consumption, though supported by tax cuts and possibly renewed declines in the saving ratio, is also likely to lose momentum as higher inflation will erode personal income gains.

With export growth weakening, real GDP growth is projected to fall short of that of domestic demand. Employment should continue to rise, however, as slower output growth can be expected to entail a deceleration in productivity gains. Assuming modest labour force growth, unemployment may experience some further decline, notably in 1987. Largely reflecting productivity developments, the growth in unit labour costs is projected to reaccelerate. The resulting upward pressure on inflation will only in part be offset by the dampening influences from the recent appreciation of sterling. Despite the projected improvement in the terms of trade, the current external account is expected to show a slightly rising deficit in the period ahead. The surplus on invisibles, which had been boosted by special factors in 1986 (lower payments abroad by North Sea companies, abnormally low net transfers to the European Community), is likely to grow at a slower pace, and the rising trend in the trade deficit is projected to be resumed, following the temporary improvement in the trade balance early this year.

57

Table 21. **Short-term prospects**

Percentage changes from previous period, seasonally adjusted annual rates

	Treasury	OECD					
	1987	1987	1988	1987		1988	
				I	II	I	II
Volumes (1980 prices)							
Private consumption	3¾	3¾	3½	3¼	4	3½	3
Government consumption	1	1½	1	¾	1	1	1
Gross fixed investment	4	2¾	3½	3	5¼	3½	1½
Public	-1	-1¾	-¾	1¾	-¾	-¾	-¾
Private	5	4¼	4½	3¼	7	4½	2¼
Final domestic demand	3¼	3¼	3	2½	3¾	3	2½
Stockbuilding[1]	¼	0	0	¼	¼	0	0
Total domestic demand	3½	3¼	3	3	3¾	3	2½
Exports	4	4½	1½	2¾	1¾	1½	1½
Imports	6	4½	4¼	-2	5¼	4¼	3½
Foreign balance[1]	-½	0	-¾	1½	-1	-¾	-½
GDP[2]	3	3¼	2¼	3½	2¾	2¼	1¾
Memorandum items:							
GDP deflator	..	4½	5¼	4¾	5¼	5½	5¼
GDP at current prices	..	8	7¾	8¼	8¼	7¾	7¼
Real personal disposable income	3½	3¾	3¼	4	3½	3	2¾
Personal saving ratio	..	11	10¾	11	10¾	10¾	10½
Consumer prices[3]	4	4	4½	4¼	4¼	4½	4½
Employment	..	1	1	1¼	1	1	¾
Unemployment rate[4]	..	11¼	11	11½	11	11	10¾
Manufacturing production	4	4¼	3¼	3½	4	3	2½
Current balance of payments							
(£ billion)	-2½	-½	-2½	0	-1	-2	-3
($ billion)	..	-1	-4½	0	-2	-3½	-5½

1. Change as a per cent of GDP in the previous period.
2. Compromise estimate of GDP at market prices for OECD and at factor cost for the Treasury.
3. Private consumption deflator for OECD and fourth quarter retail price index for the Treasury (growth rate over same period a year earlier).
4. Per cent of the labour force, including school-leavers.
Sources: *Financial Statement and Budget Report*, 1987-88 and OECD projections.

Among the risks and uncertainties surrounding the projections, the most important are certainly those related to a possible cumulative weakening in economic activity abroad. The underlying strength of the domestic economy would seem to ensure, however, continued strong activity growth in the immediate future. It is true that consumer demand has weakened somewhat and non-residential investment has failed to recover until recently. Yet, the latest quarterly survey of the Confederation of British Industry points to sharply improved business confidence, showing buoyant order, output and investment expectations. The percentage of firms reporting plant capacity as a limit to output (Diagram 12) rose by 10 percentage points between January and April 1987 and is now much higher than at the 1979 peak though still below the peak level of the 1973-74 boom. While this augurs well for higher capital spending, it may also be indicative of imminent inflationary pressures. Skilled labour shortages, on the other hand, have not changed much in the last three years and are much less pronounced than in earlier upswings (Diagram 12). Nonetheless, wage increases have remained high, especially by international comparison, and may well reaccelerate, contrary to what is assumed in the OECD's forecast. On the other hand, it cannot be excluded that the present

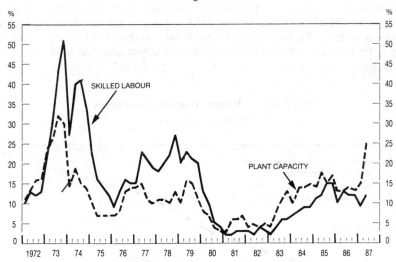

Diagram 12. **Limits on output**

Percentage balances[1]

1. Between positive and negative answers
Source: CBI, *Industrial Trends Survey.*

projections underestimate the extent to which recent productivity growth has reflected greater trend efficiency of labour rather than once-and-for-all cyclical gains. Prospects for sustained rapid growth, without inflation taking off and the external deficit widening, would, of course, be clearly improved if productivity growth held up better than assumed in the projections.

A longer-term perspective

The United Kingdom's recent growth performance compares favourably with that in the 1960s and 1970s when the economy persistently lost ground to the other industrial countries. Entering its seventh year, the current recovery is the longest in British post-war history. The rate of GDP growth achieved since 1981 has been one of the highest in the OECD area. However, as the United Kingdom economy had passed its cyclical trough earlier than many other Member countries, measuring the relative performance since the cyclical peak of 1979 may be more appropriate. Over this period, which corresponds to the Government's term of office, GDP growth averaged 1½ per cent, only slightly more than during the previous cycle and much less than during the earlier ones. This rate was well behind the performance of Japan and the United States and about the same as for OECD Europe (Diagram 13). Relatively low growth since 1979 on average reflects the depth of the recession at the beginning of the 1980s: real GDP returned to its 1979 peak only in 1983 and manufacturing output is still running a little below its 1979 level. However, this was achieved while inflation was falling by contrast to earlier periods.

While of similar size to the post-OPEC I rate, the pattern of growth since OPEC II has been very different. First, the North Sea oil contribution to output growth has been smaller. Second, productivity growth has been considerably higher (though not high by pre-1973 standards) while employment has fallen markedly. Renewed employment growth since 1983

59

has only sufficed to recuperate a little more than half of the previous losses (Diagram 13). The rise in unemployment has been reversed since mid-1986, although its rate remains at a high level by international comparison. The inflation rate, very high around the end of the 1970s, had converged to the OECD average by 1983 but a gap has persisted relative to major competitors. In spite of the high unemployment rate, wages, both nominal and real, have been rising faster than abroad, and the growth in unit labour costs has tended to outpace that

Diagram 13. **Relative economic performance**

Indices, 1979 = 100

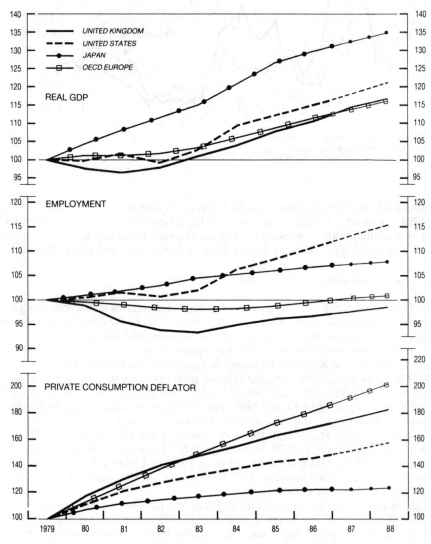

Source: OECD.

in the main trading partner countries. The manufacturing trade balance has shown a trend deterioration and, in 1983, switched into deficit for the first time since World War II. Nonetheless, the current external account was in surplus in the first half of the 1980s thanks to the exploitation of North Sea oil and gas and a rising invisibles surplus.

As noted, the Government's strategy has achieved its primary goal of bringing down the rate of inflation, although there has been little further progress in this area since 1983. It is harder to assess the respective contribution of macro- and microeconomic policies to the recovery, and in particular to the recent favourable growth performance. Increasing awareness of the distorting effects of deregulation and innovation in financial markets has led the authorities to base their judgement of monetary conditions on a wider range of indicators; this shift in emphasis would seem to have helped avoiding an unintended tightening of policy in recent years, although interest rates have remained high and have even risen in real terms. A rough indicator for the supply-side responsiveness of the economy is the split of nominal income growth as between output growth and inflation (Diagram 14). After sharply improving in the earlier part of the recovery, the output/inflation split has been broadly stable since 1983, and the 1987 MTFS projections expect little change up to 1988. This picture is confirmed by the virtual stability of a more appropriate measure, the elasticity of output to nominal aggregate demand. It should be noted, however, that in this period both the exchange rate and profit margins have adjusted to levels which would appear to be broadly sustainable in the long term, without a deterioration in the output/inflation split.

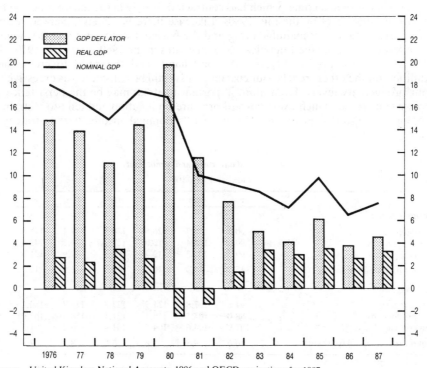

Diagram 14. **The nominal income split**

Percentage changes

Sources: *United Kingdom National Accounts,* 1986 and OECD projections for 1987.

Recent productivity gains may be indicative of an improvement in supply-side conditions, although they followed a marked activity-linked deceleration through 1985. Even so, labour productivity growth in the private business sector since 1979 was significantly higher than previously and among the highest in Member countries where it has tended to decelerate. According to OECD estimates, total factor productivity, which may be taken as an indicator for general efficiency, has risen significantly more in the present cycle than in the preceding one, contrary to developments in other major OECD countries. This result is the more noteworthy as it took place in the context of broadly similar average output growth during both cycles. The implied efficiency gains are estimated to have stemmed, with roughly equal weights, from the improvement in labour productivity growth and a deceleration in the fall of capital productivity. The former was the result of major labour shedding during the recession and early stages of the recovery, while the latter would appear to reflect accelerated scrapping of inefficient capital vintages. Both capital and labour seem to have been used more efficiently and capital/labour ratios have increased. Successful supply-side policies can be expected to raise per capita income not only by increasing the productivity of the employed but also by reducing unemployment to its frictional core. Progress has been modest in the second aspect, reflecting, among other things, persistent wage rigidity.

The failure of wages first to adjust to supply shock-induced declines in profitability and productivity trends up to the early 1980s, and then to respond to high and growing unemployment and take into account the potential disinflationary momentum of the Government's medium-term financial strategy has resulted in persistently high real labour cost growth (Table 22). This led to a massive shake-out of unprofitable labour and capital accompanied by a steep rise of labour productivity validating *ex post* the fast rise in real labour costs. As a result, adjusted for changes in the employment structure, the non-labour income share in national income, which had contracted sharply in the ten-year period to 1975, was back to its 1968 level by the mid-1980s. Likewise there has been a marked recovery of rates of return on capital in manufacturing and the business sector as a whole, though their respective levels have remained significantly below rates in the 1960s and early 1970s. In view of still relatively low profitability, on the one hand, and the need to create new job opportunities, on the other, real labour cost levels may still be considered as excessive relative to labour productivity levels. Even more important to stress may be the persistence of high *nominal* wage increases which exert upward pressure on inflation and tend to restrain output and employment growth, given the Government's nominal income-based strategy.

Table 22. **Labour costs and profitability**

Indices, 1968=100

	1965	1970	1975	1980	1985	1986	1987
Total business sector							
Real labour costs	90.5	106.7	126.8	128.1	139.4	144.8	148.9
Labour productivity	90.9	104.4	113.0	122.7	139.2	142.1	145.2
Labour cost gap	99.5	102.3	112.3	104.2	99.9	101.6	102.1
Rate of return on capital (per cent)	15.7	13.5	10.7	10.7	12.8	12.3	12.3
Manufacturing							
Real labour costs	94.6	107.8	121.9	123.8	144.7	150.2	154.5
Labour productivity	88.0	103.1	116.1	121.1	158.0	162.0	170.0
Labour cost gap	107.9	104.6	104.5	101.4	90.2	91.3	89.4
Rate of return on capital (per cent)	10.6	9.8	5.6	5.7	8.2	7.8	8.5

Source: OECD estimates and projections.

V. CONCLUSIONS

The recovery has now lasted six years, an unusually long period by post-war standards. Growth appeared to be faltering in the second half of 1985 but resumed in 1986 and prospects are good for a seventh year of expansion. The recovery was helped by the fall in the oil price, the decline in the exchange rate, and no change in policy stance following the tightening in 1985. Oil production, representing about 6 per cent of total output at prices prevailing in 1985, has levelled off, but the fall in oil prices has resulted in a switch in profitability towards energy-using companies and real pre-tax gains for consumers. In addition, consumers reduced their saving rate despite the windfall gains from lower energy prices. In view of the damping effect of oil prices on inflation and the need for some real exchange rate adjustment, continued downward pressure on sterling was not resisted. Assisted by the the fall in the exchange rate since mid-1985, export growth accelerated sharply in the second half of 1986 and has remained relatively strong in the present year, in contrast to developments in appreciating countries. At the same time, domestic demand has been supported by a decline in nominal interest rates and the resumption of growth of public expenditure on goods and services.

Recent indicators and survey results point to continued rapid activity growth in the near future. Helped by lower interest rates and income tax cuts, domestic demand should remain buoyant, with investment picking up and consumer demand remaining relatively strong. GDP growth may decelerate in 1988, however, as export performance suffers from losses in competitiveness resulting from the recent appreciation of sterling and higher cost increases than abroad. This, in turn, may adversely affect investment activity, while consumer demand is likely to weaken as a result of lower real income growth. Fiscal policy will be broadly neutral in its impact on domestic demand according to present budget plans. Nevertheless, growth performance over the next eighteen months or so should compare favourably with that of many other Member countries. There are, however, two main problems: the high rate of unemployment and the persisting inflation differential against trading partner countries. The challenge to the authorities is to ensure, through a consistent but flexible implementation of their strategy, that further improvements in the labour market are achieved while maintaining external equilibrium and downward pressure on inflation.

After a protracted period of high and rising unemployment there are signs of an improvement: the number of unemployed has been falling since mid-1986, with the share in the total of youth unemployment continuing to decline and that of long-term unemployment stabilising. These favourable trends are to some extent attributable to specific government programmes. Targeted at the young and the long-term unemployed, the measures taken entail little risk of rekindling inflation. However, while reducing social hardship and enhancing human capital, they cannot substitute for more fundamental improvements in the functioning of the labour market and, in particular the wage formation process. High unemployment has not depressed real wage growth to the same extent as in other countries. A number of measures, such as the encouragement of profit-sharing schemes, have already been taken to enhance labour market flexibility and others have been announced. The Government does not favour the use of an incomes policy, as it would be inconsistent with its goals of deregulation and greater wage differentiation. But the Government has a role to play in public sector wage settlements, and this is especially important in the light of recent increases agreed in parts of the public services.

Wages have failed to respond to the deceleration of inflation linked to the oil price fall. The underlying rate of growth of earnings has shown virtually no change since 1984. Pay settlements in the private sector have come down somewhat, but this has been largely offset by wagedrift, and settlements could now have bottomed out. Although nominal wage rigidities helped to support demand and output after the oil price fall, the more rapid increase in wages than in other countries represents a major problem. Despite improved productivity performance in the 1980s, unit labour costs have grown more than in trading partner countries. Gains in competitiveness have resulted from depreciation of sterling. While helping to maintain market shares, the fall in the exchange rate has made further progress towards price stability more difficult. Rising oil and invisibles earnings more than compensated for the widening of the deficit in the non-oil trade balance. With oil prices much lower than those prevailing in the early 1980s and oil production likely to decline, it is therefore important that wage growth should moderate so that inflation can decline further and external difficulties be avoided.

Within the framework of the Government's Medium Term Financial Strategy (MTFS), the role of monetary policy has been to reduce the rate of growth of nominal income. But as the relationship between broad money aggregates and nominal income has become increasingly less predictable — probably reflecting the fast pace of financial innovation and liberalisation — the conduct of policy has been particularly difficult in recent years. The shift in emphasis away from broad money towards other indicators has continued. The 1987 MTFS dropped the broad money target but maintained growth target ranges for the monetary base. The exchange rate has continued to play an important role in assessing monetary conditions, although it has to be interpreted alongside all other developments, including those outside the United Kingdom, such as the evolution of oil prices. One of the aims of policy, especially since the Louvre Accord, has been to avoid excessive fluctuations in the exchange rate. Given the need to allow for all these considerations, the flexible implementation of monetary policy in recent years would appear to have been relatively successful. Interest rates, although still high in nominal and real terms by international standards, have been allowed to fall considerably since 1985. Their decline was only reversed occasionally when the decrease in the exchange rate threatened to become excessive. Recently, faced with upward pressures on the exchange rate, the authorities have allowed interest rates to fall, although at a moderate pace partly because of the rapid expansion of credit.

Despite the sharp fall in oil revenues, the Public Sector Borrowing Requirement (PSBR) has come down earlier than expected to the medium-term target ratio of 1 per cent of GDP. This goal has been realised, however, at higher tax and expenditure ratios than thought desirable from the point of view of strengthening incentives in the private sector. Public revenue and expenditure as a proportion of GDP peaked in 1982 and 1984 respectively and have been on a downward trend since, but their respective shares are still above 1979 levels. The public debt/GDP ratio has declined somewhat during the course of the 1980s but, at more than 50 per cent, is still high by international standards. Moreover, as discussed in last year's Survey, the PSBR needs to be interpreted carefully in assessing the stance of fiscal policy. The public sector financial deficit (which excludes the effect of the significant step up in privatisation proceeds in recent years) has been brought down to well under 3 per cent in the last two years compared to an average of over 5 per cent in the second half of the 1970s. Over the same period, the general government financial deficit, which excludes borrowing by public corporations, fell from 4 per cent to under 3 per cent. The latter is now close to the OECD average. Although some cyclical variation in the financial deficit is appropriate, a main requirement is that it should fall further as a share of GDP over the medium term. Given the Government's intention to hold the PSBR to 1 per cent of GDP, this should occur gradually as privatisation proceeds fall as a share of GDP. In view of the present pace of GDP growth, it is important that the planned deficit in 1987/88 should not be exceeded, requiring firm control of expenditure.

The authorities have continued their efforts to improve the supply side of the economy. Major moves in this direction have already been made. It is necessary, however, to keep up the momentum by implementing wide-ranging reforms in important areas such as personal taxation, social security, local authorities and housing. Recent measures, either implemented or announced, comprise adjustments to personal taxation, tax relief on profit related pay, an expansion of employment and training measures, and a continuation of the privatisation programme. The Government has now privatised more than a third of what was the state-owned industrial sector in 1979, and there are significant further privatisations planned for the new Parliament. The programme appears to have contributed to improved profitability within both the privatised and the state-owned sector. The cumulative effect of the various measures taken so far to improve the functioning of markets can be expected to favourably influence supply-side performance over time. Yet, many rigidities remain and the impact of changes takes time to come through. Reforms should therefore be implemented without undue delays.

In the financial field major deregulation measures were taken already at the end of the 1970s. The abolition of foreign exchange controls for residents has accelerated the internationalisation of financial markets. The move towards a more market-oriented monetary policy and away from quantitative controls has been an inevitable consequence of this first step. Liberalisation measures have blurred the traditional boundaries between financial intermediaries, thereby increasing competitive pressure in domestic markets and cost efficiency of intermediation. At the same time, the task of monetary policy and of prudential control has become more complicated, given more difficult control and interpretation of monetary aggregates. Raising of capital has generally not been a constraint on real investment, with the presence of an increasing number of foreign institutions enlarging the base for business finance. Possibly worrying features are that the corporate sector has been investing to a considerable extent in financial assets rather than in physical capital and that, in relation to fixed investment, mergers and acquisitions have grown sharply. The former may be in part a consequence of the still high cost of capital relative to company profitability. The latter may be related to short-term oriented strategies of institutional investors, which have maintained a dominant position in securities markets despite official encouragement of wider share ownership.

Recent financial reforms have culminated in the complete reorganisation of the Stock Exchange, encouraged by the authorities' concern for the United Kingdom's ability to compete in domestic and international securities markets. While as an international financial centre London still ranks in the top three with New York and Tokyo, it has lost ground to other centres, with the loss in market shares most pronounced in securities trading. The removal of entry barriers and minimum commissions along with a reduction in the rate of stamp duty has led to a sharp increase in turnover and significant declines in transaction costs. The increased risk of losses and malpractices associated with the liberalisation and internationalisation of financial markets has prompted the authorities to extend the scope of formal regulation and to strengthen supervision. The new framework of financial market supervision can be characterised as controlled self-regulation. Based on functional rather than institutional lines, it may pose considerable co-ordination problems but is expected to avoid the rigidity and higher cost of more centralised systems. All in all, the reforms represent a judicious mixture of liberalisation and greater regulation of markets.

In sum, recent economic developments in the United Kingdom compare favourably both with its own past performance and that of other countries. There is no reason for complacency, however, as these appreciable developments follow upon a long period of relative decline and occur against the background of an unsatisfactory performance of other major economies. The rate of unemployment, although decreasing, is still at a high level and the external current balance is projected to deteriorate. A major problem is the stickiness of wages in the face of high unemployment. Given low inflation in other countries, wages need to adjust more if inflation is to decline further and external equilibrium is to be maintained. Continued efforts to improve supply-side conditions will facilitate the necessary adjustment process. The recovery of rates of return on capital in recent years and the apparent strengthening of total factor productivity growth may be taken as first signs that the economy is moving in the right direction.

NOTES AND REFERENCES

1. H. Rose, "Change in Financial Intermediation in the United Kingdom", *Oxford Review of Economic Policy*, Vol.2, No.4 (1986).

2. E.P. Davis, "Portfolio Behaviour of the Non-financial Private Sectors in the Major Economies", *BIS Economic Papers*, No.17 (1986).

3. "International Banking in London, 1975-85", *Bank of England Quarterly Bulletin* (September 1986).

4. "Services in the United Kingdom Economy", *Bank of England Quarterly Bulletin* (September 1985).

5. *Bank of England Quarterly Bulletin* (September 1986), *op.cit.*

6. H. Rose, *op.cit.*

7. J. Hills, "Savings and Fiscal Privilege", *Institute for Fiscal Studies*, Report Series No.9 (1984).

8. "Change in the Stock Exchange and Regulation of the City", *Bank of England Quarterly Bulletin* (February 1987).

9. *Wilson Report*, Committee to Review the Functioning of Financial Institutions, Cmnd.7937, HMSO (1980).

10. "Financial Change and Broad Money", *Bank of England Quarterly Bulletin* (December 1986).

11. C. Goodhart, "Financial Innovation and Monetary Control", *Oxford Review of Economic Policy*, Vol.2, No.4 (1986).

PRIVATISATION PROGRAMME
Privatisation sales, 1979/80 to 1986/87[1]

	£ million	
		Total
1979/80		
British Petroleum	276	
Others	94	370
1980/81		
British Aerospace	43	
North Sea Oil Licences	195	
Others	167	405
1981/82		
British Sugar Corporation (24 per cent)	44	
Cable and Wireless (49 per cent)	181	
Amersham International (100 per cent)	64	
Others	204	493
1982/83		
Britoil (51 per cent)	334	
Associated British Ports (51 per cent)	46	
International Aeradio (100 per cent)	60	
British Rail Hotels (67 per cent)	30	
North Sea Oil Licences	33	
Others	75	578
1983/84		
British Petroleum (7 per cent)	543	
Cable and Wireless (31 per cent)	263	
Britoil (41 per cent)	293	
Others	58	1 157
1984/85		
Associated British Ports (49 per cent)	51	
British Gas (Wytch Farm Oil) (100 per cent)	82	
Enterprise Oil (100 per cent)	382	
Sealink (61 per cent)	40	
Jaguar (100 per cent)	297	
National Enterprise Board Holdings	142	
North Sea Oil Licences	121	
British Telecom (34 per cent)	1 396	
Others	40	2 551
1985/86		
British Aerospace	346	
Cable and Wireless (68 per cent)	576	
Britoil (59 per cent)	426	
British Telecom	1 307	
Warship yards	54	
Others	78	2 787
1986/87[2]		
British Airways (51 per cent)	431	
British Gas (35 per cent)	1 796	
British Gas debt	750	
British Telecom (34 per cent)	1 387	
Others	125	4 489

1. Including proceeds from sales of subsidiaries from 1982/83 onwards.
2. Partly estimated.
Source: HM Treasury.

RELATIONSHIPS AMONG MONETARY AGGREGATES
AND THEIR COMPONENTS

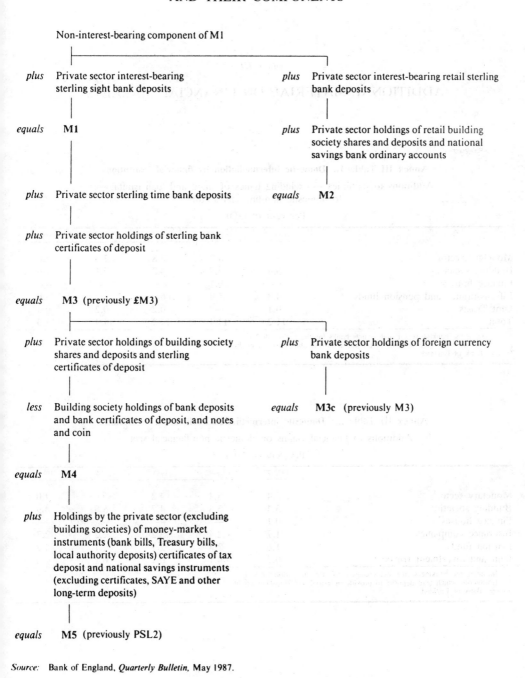

Non-interest-bearing component of M1

plus   Private sector interest-bearing   *plus*   Private sector interest-bearing retail sterling
          sterling sight bank deposits   bank deposits

equals   **M1**   *plus*   Private sector holdings of retail building
                                                     society shares and deposits and national
                                                       savings bank ordinary accounts

plus   Private sector sterling time bank deposits   *equals*   **M2**

plus   Private sector holdings of sterling bank
          certificates of deposit

equals   **M3**   (previously £M3)

plus   Private sector holdings of building society   *plus*   Private sector holdings of foreign currency
          shares and deposits and sterling   bank deposits
          certificates of deposit

less   Building society holdings of bank deposits   *equals*   **M3c**   (previously M3)
          and bank certificates of deposit, and notes
          and coin

equals   **M4**

plus   Holdings by the private sector (excluding
          building societies) of money-market
          instruments (bank bills, Treasury bills,
          local authority deposits) certificates of tax
          deposit and national savings instruments
          (excluding certificates, SAYE and other
          long-term deposits)

equals   **M5**   (previously PSL2)

Source: Bank of England, *Quarterly Bulletin,* May 1987.

Annex III

ADDITIONAL MATERIAL ON FINANCIAL MARKETS

Annex III Table 1. **Domestic intermediation by financial institutions**

Additions to liabilities — excluding issues of share and loan capital —
to domestic non-financial sectors

Per cent of GDP

	1973-77	1978-82	1983	1984	1985
Monetary sector[1]	3.3	4.7	3.8	2.8	2.6
Building societies	3.4	3.7	4.2	5.1	4.6
Finance houses[2]	—	0.1	—	—	—
Life assurance and pension funds	4.3	5.9	6.0	6.3	6.0
Unit Trusts	0.1	—	0.2	0.2	0.4
Total	11.2	14.4	14.2	14.4	13.6

1. Including the banking sector and savings banks for the period 1973-77.
2. Institutions which take deposits to provide industrial and consumer credit.
Source: Bank of England.

Annex III Table 2. **Domestic intermediation by financial institutions**

Additions to financial claims on domestic non-financial sectors

Per cent of GDP

	1973-77	1978-82	1983	1984	1985
Monetary sector[1]	5.4	5.4	4.2	5.6	4.0
Building societies	3.4	3.8	4.7	5.8	4.9
Finance houses[2]	0.1	—	—	—	—
Insurance companies	1.7	2.4	2.2	2.2	2.3
Pension funds	1.6	2.5	2.1	2.1	2.2
Unit and investment trusts	0.2	0.1	0.2	0.2	0.6

1. Including the banking sector and savings banks for the period 1973-77.
2. Institutions which take deposits to provide industrial and consumer credit.
Source: Bank of England.

Annex III Table 3. **Deposit-taking institutions: end-1978 and end-1985**

	Number of institutions		Total assets £ billion		Sterling deposit liabilities to non-bank UK residents £ billion	
	1978	1985	1978	1985	1978	1985
Monetary sector[1]	348	596	219.1	781.1	41.6	115.1
National Savings Bank	1	1				
Ordinary account			..	1.7	1.8	1.7
Investment account			1.1	5.5	1.2	5.5
Building Societies	316	167	39.7	121.2	37.0	106.9
Finance houses[2]	496	450	2.9	4.6	0.5	..

1. Banking sector before 1984. The monetary sector differs from the banking sector mainly in that it includes Trustee Savings Bank. The banking sector includes, for example, clearing banks (banks settling cheques *directly* with other clearing banks) and discount houses (financial institutions whose main business consists of discounting Treasury bills and bills of exchange).
2. Institutions which take deposits to provide industrial and consumer credit.
Source: Bank of England.

Annex III Table 4. **Investing institutions — 1978 and 1985**

£ billion

	Number at end-year		Total assets at end-year		Net inflow of funds during the year	
	1978	1985	1978	1985	1978	1985
Insurance companies[1]	810	841	46.8	151.5	4.9	17.7
Long-term funds	278	284	38.4	129.8	4.0	16.0
General funds	610	627	8.4	21.7	0.9	1.7
Pension funds[1]	4 000	4 000	31.1	157.4	3.7	24.1
Investment trusts	240	204	6.7	18.4	..	2.8
Unit trusts	414	889	3.9	19.7	0.2	4.8
Total	5 464	5 934	88.5	347.0	8.8	49.4

1. Figures include UK subsidiaries and branches of foreign companies.
Sources: *Financial Statistics* and Department of Trade and Industry.

Annex IV
CALENDAR OF MAIN ECONOMIC EVENTS

1985

16th December

Publication of White Paper on the social welfare system. The main points were:

i)   The State earnings-related pension scheme (Serps) is reprieved but its benefits are to be curtailed in order to cut its cost by the time it is fully operational twenty-five years hence;

ii)   The complex supplementary benefit and family income supplement to be replaced by the simpler income support and family credit, which will be means-tested and consistent with each other.

Implementation of most proposals will take place in April 1988.

17th December

Publication of White Paper on Banking Supervision.

19th December

Publication of Financial Services Bill containing measures to curb fraud in investment businesses through a new main regulatory authority.

1986

8th January

Major clearing banks raise base lending rates from $11\frac{1}{2}$ per cent to $12\frac{1}{2}$ per cent.

15th January

Public Expenditure White Paper (Cmnd.9703) published. The main points were:

i)   Estimates for the public expenditure planning total for 1986/87 and 1987/88 were projected at £139 billion and £144 billion, respectively, as in the March 1985 Financial Statement and Budget Report. A planning total of £149 billion was set for 1988/89;

ii)   The cash plans mean that public spending between 1985/86 and 1988/89 should remain broadly stable in real terms and fall in relation to nominal income;

iii)   Cuts are planned in expenditure on defence and social security, while assets sales are being substantially stepped up.

20th January

Statutory sick pay rates to be increased by 5.4 per cent from 6th April.

28th January

Publication of Green Paper «Paying for Local Government» (Cmnd.9714), detailing radical reforms of the rates system.

6th February

Publication of White Paper «Privatisation of the Water Authorities in England and Wales», (Cmnd. 9734).

18th March

The Budget introduced to Parliament. Main points were:

i)   Income tax: basic rate down 1 per cent to 29 per cent; personal allowances indexed: single person's allowance up £130 to £2 335 and married person's allowance up £200 to £3 665; higher-rate thresholds up by £1 000; age allowances up £160 for a single person, £250 for a married couple;

ii)   Tobacco duty: up 11p a packet on cigarettes, no change in cigar and pipe tobacco duty; fuel duty: petrol up 7½p a gallon;

iii)   VAT threshold to rise from £19 500 to £20 500 a year;

iv)   Stamp duty halved to 0.5 per cent on share deals;

v)   Small investors' tax incentives (Personal Equity Plans) introduced for regular share-buying of up to £2 400 a year;

vi)   Corporation tax down 5 per cent for large firms to 35 per cent and down 1 per cent to 29 per cent for smaller ones;

vii)   Employment measures: Community Programme for long-term unemployed to be increased by 55 000 places, from 200 000, and average wage up from £63 to £67 a week; Job Start Scheme to be expanded from nine pilot areas to nationwide; Enterprise Allowance Scheme to be expanded from 65 000 to 100 000 entrants a year; Business Expansion Scheme to be extended indefinitely; Small Firms Loan Guarantee Scheme to be extended for three years, with premium halved from 5 per cent to 2½ per cent; A New Workers Scheme to help young people during their first year into jobs by providing subsidy of £15 a week to employers recruiting 18-19 year-olds at less than £55 and 20 year-olds at below £65 a week. The employment measures will cost £100 million net in 1986/87 and £165 million in 1987/88;

viii)   Social Security benefits' increases for old-age pensioners and widows payable in July to be tax-exempt in 1986/87, at a cost of £15 million;

ix)   PSBR for 1986/87 set at £7 billion, or 1¾ per cent of GDP. Target range for £M3 growth for 1986/87 is 11 to 15 per cent and for M0 2 to 6 per cent.

19th March

Major clearing banks reduce base lending rates from 12½ per cent to 11½ per cent. Two major building societies, Halifax and Abbey National, cut rates on mortgage repayment from 12¾ per cent to 12 per cent.

20th March

Other building societies cut rates on mortgage repayment from 12¾ per cent to 12 per cent.

8th April

Major clearing banks reduce base lending rates from 11½ per cent to 11 per cent.

18th April

Major clearing banks reduce base lending rates from 11 per cent to 10½ per cent.

21st April

Leading building societies cut mortgage rates from 11 per cent to 10½ per cent.

22nd May

National Westminster Bank reduces base lending rate from 10½ per cent to 10 per cent.

23rd May

Other major clearing banks reduce base lending rates from 10½ per cent to 10 per cent.

17th June

Indefinite postponement of the privatisation of Royal Ordnance.

5th August

Oil prices up by $5 to $15 a barrel as OPEC announces measures to cut production over following two months from 20 mbd. to 16.8 mbd.

3rd September

Government borrows $4 billion (£2.7 billion) on the international markets to replenish official reserves.

24th September

Flotation of Trustee Savings Bank.

14th October

Bank of England and major clearing banks raise base lending rates from 10 per cent to 11 per cent.

21st October

Halifax Building Society to raise mortgage rate from 11 per cent to $12\frac{1}{4}$ per cent from 1st November.

22nd October

OPEC agrees to limit oil production until the end of 1986.

27th October

London's Stock Exchange changes over to electronic trading and information systems — the *Big Bang*.

31st October

Spot price of Brent crude oil up $1 to $14.9 a barrel.

6th November

Autumn Statement by the Chancellor of the Exchequer. Main points were:
  i)   Public expenditure up by £4.7 billion in 1987/88 and £5.5 billion in 1988/89, mainly on education, social security, health and law and order;
  ii) Asset sales to raise £5 billion in each of the next financial years;
  iii) PSBR projection for 1986/87 remains at £7 billion.

7th November

Publication of Financial Services Act, 1986, to regulate the conduct of investment business by replacing investor protection legislation and extending the scope of formal regulation.

21st December

OPEC decides to limit oil output to 15.8 mbd. for the first half of 1987 and to fix prices.

1987

15th January

Public Expenditure White Paper published. Main points were:
  i)   General government expenditure is projected to increase by 1 per cent per year in real terms between 1986/87 and 1989/90, with much of the increase allocated to education, health, law and order.
  ii) General government expenditure (excluding privatisation proceeds) is projected to fall as a proportion of GDP from $44\frac{1}{2}$ per cent in 1986/87 to $42\frac{1}{4}$ per cent by 1989/90.

74

9th March

Major clearing banks reduce their base lending rates from 11 per cent to $10\frac{1}{2}$ per cent.

17th March

The Budget introduced to Parliament. Main points were:

   i)   The basic rate of income tax reduced to 27 per cent; the main personal allowances for income tax relief raised in line with inflation (3.7 per cent): single person's earned income allowance raised by £90 to £2 425 and married person's allowance up £140 to £3 795; higher age thresholds up by £110 for single persons and £170 for a married couple;

   ii)   Income tax relief introduced for employees in profit-related pay schemes (PRP) under certain conditions and up to a maximum amount of £3 000 or 20 per cent of PAYE pay, whichever is the lower;

   iii) Major excise duties rates not adjusted for inflation at an estimated cost of £455 million in 1987/88 and at £490 million in 1988/89 (from an indexed base);

   iv) The small companies' rate of corporation tax reduced from 29 per cent to 27 per cent. The main rate for corporation tax remains at 35 per cent;

   v)   New tax regime for personal pensions introduced in 1988. Employees will be able to contract-out of the SERPS by joining a personal pension scheme to which the DHSS will pay a minimum contribution;

   vi) Tax treatment of members of Lloyd's to be put in line with that of ordinary insurance companies, which affects Lloyd's reinsurance activity;

   vii) VAT registration limit to be £21 300 per annum; notification period extended to thirty days and collection of system to be modified to assist small businesses;

   vii) PSBR target set at £4 billion in 1987/88 and 1988/89 and £5 billion in the two following fiscal years, or 1 per cent of GDP. The projections allow for a fiscal adjustment of £3 billion in 1988/89 and £2 billion in 1989/90 and 1990/91;

   ix) Target range for M0 growth set at 2 to 6 per cent in 1987/88. No formal target for £M3 in 1987/88.

19th March

Major clearing banks reduce their base lending rates from $10\frac{1}{2}$ per cent to 10 per cent.

28th April

Major clearing banks reduce their base lending rates from 10 per cent to $9\frac{1}{2}$ per cent.

8th May

Major clearing banks reduce their base lending rates from $9\frac{1}{2}$ per cent to 9 per cent.

11th May

The Government announces a number of new measures to strengthen the powers of the self-regulatory Panel on Take-overs and Mergers without, however, bringing them within a statutory framework.

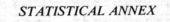

STATISTICAL ANNEX

Table A. Expenditure on GDP
£ million

	GDP at factor cost*	Final expenditure at market prices**	Total domestic demand***	Consumers' expenditure	Public current expenditure	Fixed investment	Change in stocks	Exports of goods and services	Imports of goods and services	Indirect taxes less subsidies
	1	2	3	4	5	6	7	8	9	10
At current prices:										
1982	235 362	344 263	271 203	167 382	60 480	44 647	−1 306	73 060	68 122	40 779
1983	258 017	378 401	298 002	182 600	65 939	48 812	651	80 399	77 580	42 804
1984	275 048	412 243	320 345	195 341	69 787	55 577	−360	91 898	92 445	44 750
1985	302 368	450 265	347 949	213 235	74 101	60 068	545	102 316	98 786	49 111
1986	318 659	474 222	376 313	231 632	79 820	64 017	844	97 909	100 844	54 719
At 1980 prices...										
1977	194 382	274 694	215 083	124 868	46 172	41 441	2 602	59 611	52 177	28 135
1978	199 514	284 649	223 914	131 742	47 238	42 726	2 208	60 735	54 203	30 932
1979	203 805	295 489	232 326	137 612	48 213	43 954	2 547	63 163	59 879	31 805
1980	199 606	288 197	225 100	137 234	48 936	41 774	−2 844	63 097	57 868	30 723
1981	197 850	284 352	221 616	137 220	49 042	37 844	−2 490	62 736	56 404	30 098
1982	199 488	289 395	226 125	138 285	49 563	39 404	−1 127	63 270	59 484	30 423
1983	207 007	301 234	236 560	143 610	50 530	41 740	680	64 674	62 773	31 454
1984	210 931	312 133	243 002	146 667	50 896	45 490	−51	69 131	68 558	32 644
1985	218 355	323 023	249 886	151 961	50 993	46 328	604	73 137	70 691	33 977
1986	223 433	333 231	257 918	159 165	51 587	46 602	564	75 313	74 826	34 972
...and seasonally adjusted:										
1985 1	54 458	80 501	62 312	37 448	12 712	12 123	29	18 189	17 686	8 357
2	54 574	80 466	61 952	37 597	12 790	11 172	393	18 514	17 501	8 391
3	54 527	80 625	62 639	38 295	12 711	11 571	62	17 986	17 496	8 602
4	54 796	81 431	62 983	38 621	12 780	11 462	120	18 448	18 008	8 627
1986 1	55 855	82 108	64 082	38 977	12 768	11 803	534	18 026	17 706	8 547
2	55 546	82 364	63 734	39 610	12 768	11 485	−141	18 630	18 154	8 664
3	55 627	83 623	64 819	40 280	13 003	11 804	−268	18 804	19 165	8 831
4	56 405	85 136	65 283	40 298	13 036	11 510	439	19 853	19 801	8 930

Note: For the years prior to 1978 the aggregates differ slightly from the sum of the components due to the method of rebasing to 1980 prices.
*   1 = 2−9−10.
**   2 = 4+5+6+7+8.
*** 3 = 2−8.
Source: Economic Trends.

Table B. **Gross domestic fixed capital formation**
£ million at 1980 prices, seasonally adjusted

	Total	Private sector[1]	General government[1]	Public corporations[1]	Vehicles, ships and aircraft	Plant and machinery	Dwellings		Other new building and works[2]	Extraction of mineral oil and natural gas	Manufacturing[3]
							Private	Public			
1977	41 441	26 510	7 555	7 285	4 722	13 001	5 560	3 382	14 777	3 319	6 774
1978	42 726	29 201	6 718	6 807	5 187	13 928	5 934	3 114	14 563	3 088	7 221
1979	43 954	30 732	6 423	6 799	5 446	15 010	6 468	2 893	14 137	2 525	7 496
1980	41 774	29 641	5 498	6 635	4 577	14 978	6 116	2 559	13 544	2 399	6 478
1981	37 844	27 739	4 060	6 045	3 549	13 901	5 454	1 720	13 220	2 680	4 865
1982	39 404	29 482	3 788	6 134	3 653	14 119	5 457	1 827	14 348	2 763	4 704
1983	41 740	29 966	5 174	6 600	3 750	14 772	6 075	2 342	14 801	2 584	4 780
1984	45 490	33 675	5 790	6 025	4 369	16 064	6 616	2 251	16 190	2 798	5 762
1985	46 328	36 204	5 613	4 511	4 680	17 388	6 415	1 994	15 851	2 335	5 852
1986	46 602	36 282	6 170	4 150	4 170	17 216	7 263	2 025	15 928	2 001	5 818
1985 1	12 123	9 579	1 294	1 250	1 456	4 627	1 574	526	3 940	634	1 500
2	11 172	8 659	1 382	1 131	1 121	4 018	1 590	480	3 963	550	1 423
3	11 571	8 987	1 451	1 133	1 105	4 350	1 621	503	3 992	610	1 447
4	11 462	8 979	1 486	997	998	4 393	1 630	485	3 956	541	1 482
1986 1	11 803	9 071	1 617	1 115	1 025	4 441	1 614	580	4 143	523	1 482
2	11 485	8 928	1 545	1 012	1 085	4 266	1 796	485	3 853	470	1 456
3	11 804	9 289	1 471	1 044	1 033	4 298	1 991	478	4 004	544	1 463
4	11 510	8 994	1 537	979	1 027	4 211	1 862	482	3 928	464	1 417

Note: For the years prior to 1978, totals differ slightly from the sums of their components due to the method of rebasing to 1980 prices.
1. Including purchases less sales of land and existing buildings.
2. Including transfer costs of land and buildings.
3. Including leased assets.
Source: Economic Trends.

Table C. Consumption and investment
Seasonally adjusted

	Consumer demand				Investment					
	Total retail sales	Non-food retail sales	New car registrations	Changes in hire purchase debt total[1]	Capital expenditure of		Engineering new home orders[2]	Housing starts		Investment in stocks (manufacturing)
					Manufacturing industry	Distribution and services industries		Private	Public	
	Volume, 1980 = 100		Thousands, monthly averages	£ million, end of period	£ million at 1980 prices		Average monthly sales 1980 = 100	Thousands		£ million at 1980 prices
1976	93.1	93.9	107	348	6 475	9 827	95	154.7	170.8	437
1977	91.5	92.1	109	935	6 774	10 613	100	134.8	132.1	1 354
1978	96.4	99.3	132	1 547	7 221	11 581	112	157.3	107.4	476
1979	100.6	103.8	142	1 402	7 495	12 709	108	144.0	81.2	275
1980	100.0	100.0	127	937	6 479	12 808	92	98.9	56.4	−2 321
1981	100.2	99.7	125	627	4 865	12 123	95	116.7	37.2	−1 516
1982	102.1	101.9	132	1 446	4 705	12 539	93	140.5	52.8	−1 113
1983 1	105.4	105.7	146	546	1 117	3 173	87	45.5	14.9	38
2	106.6	107.6	147	430	1 165	3 208	94	41.7	11.7	−65
3	107.7	108.2	158	601	1 207	3 232	100	40.6	9.7	−274
4	109.0	110.3	151	669	1 290	3 515	101	42.0	11.3	169
1984 1	109.0	108.2	147	619	1 385	3 378	104	40.4	12.1	105
2	111.0	111.2	150	614	1 421	3 747	103	38.6	10.1	−59
3	111.8	112.4	148	413	1 447	3 943	102	38.1	9.7	105
4	113.5	114.0	141	513	1 502	4 000	103	36.6	8.3	150
1985 1	114.4	113.8	148	586	1 498	4 660	104	36.9	8.2	−216
2	115.9	115.6	151	533	1 424	3 902	100	40.0	8.4	215
3	117.3	116.8	157	745	1 447	4 134	101	41.3	8.1	−21
4	117.9	117.9	158	722	1 481	4 060	110	43.6	8.9	−463
1986 1	119.3	118.7	146	980	1 483	4 213	111	40.7	7.7	−177
2	121.3	128.5	155	418	1 455	4 048	111	42.5	7.5	68
3	123.7	131.7	162	968	1 461	4 030	111	45.6	8.3	−51
4	126.5	135.3	159	586	1 441	4 009	107	43.3	7.9	−99
1987 1	125.4	132.4	158	1 117	..	..	..	49.4	6.7	:
% Change latest quarter:										
on previous quarter	−0.9	−2.1	−0.6		−1.4	−0.5				
on a year earlier	5.1	11.5	8.2		−2.7	−1.3				

1. Up to 1979, including further interest payments due over the whole period of the loans.
2. Net of cancellations.
Sources: *Economic Trends* and *Monthly Digest of Statistics*.

Table D. Production and manpower
Seasonally adjusted

	GDP compromise estimate[1]	GDP per person employed[2]	Index of industrial production	Index of manufacturing production	Unemployed[3]	Unfilled vacancies adults	Employment in whole economy	Employment in manufacturing industries	Hours of overtime worked in manufacturing industries
	1980 = 100				Thousands		1980 = 100		Million per week
1976	94.4	95.0	95.2	106.9	1 179	122	98.7	107.4	14.01
1977	97.0	97.6	100.1	108.9	1 251	155	99.0	107.7	15.58
1978	99.6	100.4	103.1	109.5	1 226	210	99.4	106.1	15.61
1979	102.3	102.2	107.1	109.5	1 140	241	100.6	105.3	15.07
1980	100.0	100.0	100.0	100.0	1 452	134	100.0	100.0	11.76
1981	98.8	101.9	96.6	94.0	2 270	91	96.6	91.0	9.37
1982	100.3	105.8	98.4	94.2	2 626	114	94.6	85.5	9.93
1983 1	102.7	108.7	100.3	95.8	2 804	124	93.5	82.1	9.68
2	102.8	109.1	100.6	95.4	2 865	133	93.5	81.2	9.60
3	104.1	110.7	102.8	97.5	2 890	145	93.9	80.6	10.59
4	105.1	111.3	104.0	98.9	2 906	148	94.4	80.1	11.24
1984 1	105.9	111.3	104.0	99.4	2 949	147	94.9	79.8	11.20
2	105.6	111.2	102.6	100.3	2 973	149	95.2	79.8	11.59
3	106.9	111.5	102.4	101.4	3 017	151	95.7	79.9	11.58
4	108.0	111.9	103.7	101.7	3 055	153	96.2	79.8	11.86
1985 1	109.2	113.0	106.4	103.3	3 088	156	96.6	79.7	11.88
2	110.6	114.1	109.3	104.5	3 119	162	96.9	79.7	11.76
3	110.4	113.8	108.1	103.5	3 124	163	97.2	79.6	12.09
4	110.7	114.4	108.4	103.6	3 122	167	97.3	79.5	12.19
1986 1	111.9	114.9	109.1	102.6	3 171	167	97.3	79.1	11.84
2	112.6	116.0	109.2	103.5	3 208	176	97.4	78.5	11.50
3	113.4	117.4	110.8	104.8	3 212	200	97.6	77.8	11.67
4	114.5	117.7	110.7	107.1	3 143	213	97.9	77.7	11.85
1987 1	..	..	112.2	106.9	3 077	209	..	77.4	11.89
% change latest quarter: on previous quarter			+1.4	-0.2			+0.3	-0.4	+0.3
on a year earlier			+2.8	+4.2			+0.6	-2.1	+0.4

1. Average of expenditure, income and output data.
2. Based on output-based GDP.
3. United Kingdom, excluding school leavers.
Sources: *Economic Trends* and *Department of Employment Gazette*.

Table E. Domestic finance
Seasonally adjusted

	Change in narrow money supply M1	Change in money supply Sterling M3	General government borrowing requirement	Sterling lending to the private sector by banks	Net increase in building society shares and deposits	Building society new commitments to mortgages	Government securities-calculated redemption yields[1]			Local authority deposits 3 months rates*	Covered comparison between local authority and Euro-dollar 3 months rates[2]
							Short-dated	Medium-dated	Long-dated		
	£ million				£ million		% per annum			% per annum at end of period	
1976	1 944	3 528	8 938	3 407	3 405	6 090	12.06	13.61	14.43	14.88	−0.41
1977	2 189	4 127	5 463	3 188	6 099	7 254	10.08	12.02	12.73	6.73	0.16
1978	3 841	6 737	8 436	4 698	4 822	8 710	11.32	12.07	12.47	12.44	−0.33
1979	2 492	6 651	12 681	8 585	5 769	9 119	12.67	12.95	12.99	17.22	0.32
1980	1 203	10 610	11 822	10 025	7 159	10 228	13.84	13.91	13.78	14.75	0.34
1981	3 138	9 342	10 590	11 192	7 196	11 948	14.65	14.88	14.74	15.75	0.60
1982	4 398	7 477	4 954	17 769	6 466	16 899	12.79	13.08	12.88	10.63	0.13
1983 1	1 409	3 769	4 438	1 610	1 292	5 049	11.29	11.68	11.36	10.75	0.22
2	1 003	2 382	1 765	3 608	1 261	4 448	11.07	11.07	10.53	9.69	0.03
3	915	1 036	2 502	4 135	2 002	4 583	11.55	11.50	10.90	9.69	0.04
4	1 244	2 252	2 923	3 550	2 316	5 229	10.86	10.82	10.42	9.31	0.10
1984 1	2 156	2 022	2 467	4 272	2 732	5 855	10.59	10.77	10.31	8.94	−0.05
2	1 960	2 791	3 282	3 179	2 063	6 729	11.30	11.41	10.83	9.50	0.08
3	1 669	2 568	2 585	3 948	1 664	6 146	12.17	11.85	11.14	10.75	0.05
4	1 092	2 569	1 879	5 142	2 113	5 901	11.10	11.05	10.49	10.13	0.29
1985 1	2 335	3 857	2 380	6 179	1 700	6 201	11.70	11.60	10.98	13.13	0.13
2	2 179	2 941	1 194	4 952	1 921	6 471	11.35	11.23	10.75	12.56	0.21
3	2 819	4 715	2 369	4 511	1 944	7 047	10.78	10.73	10.40	11.38	0.08
4	1 931	2 974	1 572	5 326	1 897	8 044	10.69	10.69	10.35	11.94	0.08
1986 1	3 355	8 155	1 600	6 270	2 448	8 044	10.86	10.57	10.20	11.25	−0.73
2	4 140	6 934	928	6 510	1 762	10 581	8.57	8.89	9.00	9.75	−0.01
3	5 310	6 186	2 453	6 899	219	10 661	9.50	9.69	9.58	10.38	0.02
4	−222	2 327	−2 771	10 514	2 206	8 247	11.13	11.06	10.70	11.31	0.25
1987 1	5 689	10 196	1 469	6 640	1 652	7 996	9.73	9.77	9.69	9.87	−0.03

* Not seasonally adjusted.
1. Average of wednesday yields until February 1980; from March 1980 figures are the average of all observations (3 a week); from January 1982, figures are the average of working days.
2. Difference between the local authority rate net of the cost of forward cover and the Euro-dollar rate. A plus indicates that the net local authority rate is above the Euro-dollar rate and a minus that it is below.

Sources: *Bank of England Quarterly Bulletin and Financial Statistics.*

Table F. Wages, prices and external position
Seasonally adjusted

	Average earnings[1]	Producer prices manufacturing output for home market*[2]	Retail prices*	Export unit values*	Import unit values*	Exports (fob)	Imports (fob)	Visible balance	Current balance	Official financing*
	January 1980 = 100	1980 = 100	1975 = 100	1980 = 100	1980 = 100	£ million	£ million			£ million
1976	65.1	60.9	116.6	60.8	70.9	25 191	29 120	−3 929	−920	−3 629
1977	71.0	72.0	135.1	72.0	82.1	31 728	34 012	−2 284	−136	7 362
1978	80.2	79.1	146.2	79.1	85.2	35 063	36 605	−1 542	965	−1 126
1979	92.6	87.7	165.8	87.6	90.9	40 687	44 136	−3 449	−717	1 905
1980	111.4	100.0	195.6	100.0	100.0	47 422	46 061	1 361	2 929	1 372
1981	125.8	109.5	218.8	108.8	108.2	50 977	47 617	3 360	6 159	−687
1982	137.6	118.0	237.6	116.2	116.7	55 565	53 234	2 331	3 936	−1 284
1983 1	146.0	121.8	242.6	123.0	125.1	14 682	14 613	69	1 579	−616
2	147.9	124.2	247.5	124.9	126.7	14 745	15 210	−465	−49	129
3	150.4	125.1	250.7	126.9	127.7	15 290	15 376	−86	1 153	−5
4	152.5	126.8	253.5	128.2	130.4	16 059	16 412	−353	452	−328
1984 1	154.9	129.0	255.1	131.4	133.9	16 693	16 706	−13	1 249	−190
2	155.9	132.0	260.3	134.3	137.6	16 855	18 124	−1 269	−343	−668
3	159.1	132.8	262.5	137.1	141.4	17 628	19 144	−1 516	−158	−343
4	163.3	134.5	265.8	141.3	145.8	19 191	20 277	−1 086	534	−115
1985 1	166.8	136.6	269.2	146.4	152.3	20 081	21 279	−1 198	−115	−274
2	170.2	139.4	278.4	145.5	148.7	20 192	20 404	−212	1 302	438
3	173.9	140.2	279.1	141.7	141.4	18 703	19 299	−596	1 147	−32
4	176.1	141.4	280.5	140.5	138.3	19 135	19 307	−172	612	667
1986 1	180.6	143.3	282.5	139.0	137.6	18 164	19 391	−1 227	682	351
2	184.1	145.7	286.1	134.8	131.5	17 786	19 337	−1 551	−94	426
3	186.9	146.3	286.5	134.3	130.2	17 553	20 426	−2 873	−931	1 719
4	190.1	147.4	290.1	138.1	137.0	19 339	21 942	−2 603	−757	..
1987 1	..	149.3	293.7	140.7	140.0	19 534	20 710	−1 176	625	..
% of change latest quarter:										
on previous quarter	+1.7	+1.3	+1.2	+1.9	+2.2					
on a year earlier	+7.9	+4.2	+4.0	+1.2	+1.7					

* Not seasonally adjusted.
1. From 1973 to 1975 index, january 1970 = 100 and from 1976 to 1979 index, january 1976 = 100 linked to index january 1980 = 100.
2. Excluding food, drink, tobacco.
Sources: *Economic Trends* and *Employment Gazette.*

83

Table G. Net capital transactions
Not seasonally adjusted, £ million

	Current balance	UK investment overseas			Lending overseas by UK banks			Lending overseas by UK residents other than banks and general government			Other external government transactions	Total investment and other capital transactions	Drawings on (+) or additions to (−) reserves	Allocation of SDR'S and gold subs- cription to IMF	Balancing item
		Total	Direct	Portfolio	Total	Foreign currency	Sterling	Total	Public corpora- tions	Non bank private sector					
1975	−1 582	329	194	135	666	545	121	902	286	616	−951	946	655	—	−19
1976	−920	355	−767	1 122	−708	322	−1 030	542	822	−280	−448	−259	853	—	326
1977	−136	2 069	147	1 922	2 265	1 041	1 224	1 277	958	319	736	6 347	−9 588	—	3 377
1978	965	−2 770	−1 558	−1 212	−2 022	−1 049	−973	227	134	93	−886	−5 451	2 329	—	2 157
1979	−717	−2 219	−2 859	640	3 548	550	2 998	−7	150	−157	−332	990	−1 059	195	591
1980	2 969	−2 300	−569	731	729	495	234	−832	5	−837	−242	−2 645	−291	180	−173
1981	6 159	−7 138	−3 161	−3 977	−891	401	−490	−787	−262	−525	−113	−8 929	2 419	158	193
1982	3 936	−7 853	−1 358	−6 495	3 767	3 365	402	−98	−232	134	246	−3 938	1 421	—	−1 419
1983	3 135	−6 495	−1 863	−4 632	2 804	1 090	1 714	−529	−67	−462	−1 054	−5 274	607	—	1 532
1984	1 282	−13 683	−5 552	−8 161	10 702	9 502	1 200	−3 547	−49	−3 498	−792	−7 320	908	—	5 130
1985 1	−115	−5 633	−990	−4 643	3 012	1 718	1 294	−673	−10	−663	−29	−3 323	90	—	3 991
2	1 302	−3 207	−937	−2 270	1 194	1 132	62	1 442	35	1 407	−139	−710	−607	—	416
3	1 147	−3 505	−750	−2 755	−2 154	−3 307	1 153	653	97	556	−80	−5 086	−49	—	3 878
4	612	−2 456	−923	−1 533	5 361	5 357	4	1 106	−114	1 220	−461	−3 550	−1 192	—	−3 904
1986 1	682	−2 438	1 301	−3 739	2 614	791	1 823	−1 018	−141	−877	247	−595	−580	—	999
2	−94	−4 836	−64	−4 772	1 486	2 880	−1 394	1 286	−18	1 304	−28	−2 092	−296	—	2 895
3	−931	−4 048	−1 524	−2 524	5 282	6 010	−728	2 093	3	2 090	2	−3 329	−2 321	—	111
4	−757	−4 058	−3 609	−449	653	849	−196	459	−33	492	−563	−3 509	306	—	2 853

Source: Economic Trends.

84

Table H. Foreign assets and liabilities

	Effective exchange rate 1970Q1 = 100	Official reserves[1] Total	of which: Convertible currencies	Sterling balances Official Total	of which: Oil-exporting countries	Sterling balances Other holders	Outstanding official borrowing from abroad[2] Total	of which: IMF[3]
		$ million, end of period	$ million, end of period	£ million, end of period	£ million, end of period	£ million, end of period	$ million, end of period	$ million, end of period
1976	64.9	4 129	2 513	2 647	1 421	3 484	14 199	1 975
1977	61.8	20 557	19 015	2 852	1 360	4 965	18 365	4 057
1978	62.4	15 694	14 230	2 633	1 006	5 258	16 508	2 324
1979	65.6	22 538	18 034	3 320	1 205	7 838	14 753	1 071
1980	72.5	27 476	18 621	4 669	2 238	10 309	12 012	717
1981	74.8	23 347	13 457	4 757	2 471	12 916	8 239	364
1982	71.9	16 997	9 634	5 561	2 654	17 530	7 893	57
1983	67.3	17 817	9 040	6 628	2 758	21 408	8 023	–
1984 1	66.6	16 749	8 465	7 040	2 720	22 756	8 263	–
2	65.1	15 505	7 063	7 213	2 615	24 701	7 874	–
3	64.3	15 260	7 032	7 437	2 796	26 297	7 808	–
4	62.3	15 694	7 577	7 755	2 702	26 825	8 271	–
1985 1	60.7	13 528	6 818	7 572	2 444	31 783	8 505	–
2	66.1	14 318	7 560	7 872	2 614	31 719	8 755	–
3	68.2	14 176	7 351	8 395	2 534	31 972	9 077	–
4	66.2	15 543	8 486	9 327	3 099	31 236	11 861	–
1986 1	61.9	18 750	10 650	9 738	3 277	34 617	12 343	–
2	62.7	19 188	11 082	9 155	3 121	34 644	12 242	–
3	59.0	22 426	14 435	9 367	3 331	35 371	16 362	–
4	55.7	21 923	13 781	9 409	3 522	37 199	..	..
1987 1	56.7	27 039	..	..	..	..	..	..

Memorandum item: Schedule of capital repayments of certain public sector foreign currency liabilities outstanding at end-1981 ($ billion).

1982	1983	1984	1985	1986	1987	1988	1989	1990	1991	1992 onwards	Total
1.7	0.9	1.6	1.2	1.2	1.4	1.2	0.9	0.7	0.7	2.8	14.3

1. From end-March 1979 the rates at which the reserves are valued are to be revised annually. Gold is valued at $35 per fine ounce until end-November 1971, then at $38 per fine ounce until end-January 1973 and at $42.2222 per fine ounce until end-March 1979. Special drawing rights are valued at SDR 1=$1 until end-November 1971, then at SDR 1=$1.08571 until end-January 1973 and at SDR 1=$1.20635 to end-March 1979. Convertible currencies are valued at middle or central rates from end-December 1971 to end-March 1979. The basis of valuation announced in 1979 was modified in March 1980. In 1979, gold was valued at the average of the London fixing price for the three months up to end-March, less 25%; from end-March 1980 it is to be valued at that price or at 75% of its final fixing price on the last working day in March, whichever is the lower. US dollar rates against the US dollar in the three months to end-March 1979 at the average of their exchange rates against the US dollar in the three months to end-March, with the alternative from end-March 1980, of their value on the last working day of March, whichever is lower, convertible currencies include European currency units (ECUs) acquired from swaps with the European Monetary Co-operation Fund. These are valued at the average of the $/ECU or $/European unit of account exchange rates in the three months to end-March or (from end-March 1980) at the rate applicable on the last working day in March, whichever is lower. Until March 1980 this valuation differed from that used for monthly reserve announcements, where ECUs were valued at the market rate applicable for each swap.
2. The borrowing included is that recorded as official financing in the balance of payments accounts. From end-March 1979 the rates at which outstanding borrowing is valued are to be revised annually on the same basis at the reserves. The effect of the 1979 revaluation was to increase the level of borrowings at end-March by $576 million (IMF +$148 million and other public sector +$428 million).
3. Drawings from the IMF, net of repayments by the United Kingdom, and drawings of sterling from the IMF by other countries; excludes interest and charges in sterling.
Source: *Bank of England Quarterly Bulletin.*

Table I. Foreign trade by area

Million US dollars, monthly averages

	1972	1973	1974	1975	1976	1977	1978	1979	1980	1981	1982	1983	1984	1985	1986
Imports, cif															
Total OECD	1 660	2 308	3 021	3 082	3 231	3 775	4 951	6 637	7 564	6 708	6 614	6 810	7 156	7 604	8 831
North America	372	482	631	592	635	716	854	1 100	1 452	1 272	1 183	1 141	1 231	1 264	1 228
OECD Europe	1 111	1 610	2 169	2 264	2 368	2 798	3 766	5 117	5 604	4 931	4 892	5 114	5 384	5 758	6 867
EEC	738	1 071	1 518	1 642	1 725	2 055	2 670	3 721	4 060	3 628	3 684	3 805	3 920	4 207	5 444
Centrally planned economies	84	115	136	129	161	183	191	250	253	141	168	166	198	172	188
Developing countries	511	723	1 251	1 127	1 204	1 211	1 271	1 567	2 026	1 582	1 393	1 246	1 309	1 368	1 444
of which: OPEC	209	295	724	575	611	528	538	580	826	603	482	331	286	277	202
Exports, fob															
Total OECD	1 427	1 831	2 278	2 410	2 650	3 293	4 081	5 526	6 941	6 090	5 840	5 720	6 010	6 635	6 911
North America	333	395	440	426	465	555	678	854	1 055	1 204	1 216	1 181	1 270	1 438	1 482
OECD Europe	961	1 264	1 610	1 762	1 989	2 517	3 135	4 361	5 562	4 595	4 325	4 283	4 464	4 897	5 091
EEC	626	843	1 094	1 204	1 403	1 783	2 290	3 210	4 081	3 569	3 372	3 352	3 515	3 911	4 284
Centrally planned economies	61	70	89	115	105	126	161	179	229	175	135	125	153	134	151
Developing countries	473	558	735	996	1 019	1 275	1 609	1 710	2 206	2 126	1 932	1 649	1 539	1 677	1 802
of which: OPEC	119	147	213	380	431	565	703	603	881	932	850	666	561	555	578

Source: OCDE, Foreign Trade Statistics.

BASIC STATISTICS :

INTERNATIONAL COMPARISONS

	Units	Reference period[1]	Australia	Aust
Population				
Total	Thousands	1985	15 752	7 555
Inhabitants per sq.km	Number		2	90
Net average annual increase over previous 10 years	%		1.3	0.0
Employment				
Total civilian employment (TCE)[2]	Thousands	1985	6 676	3 235
of which: Agriculture	% of TCE		6.2	9.0
Industry	% of TCE		27.7	38.1
Services	% of TCE		66.1	52.9
Gross domestic product (GDP)				
At current prices and current exchange rates	Billion US$	1985	155.1	66.1
Per capita	US$		9 847	8 743
At current prices using current PPP's[3]	Billion US$	1984	..	85.7
Per capita	US$		..	11 345
Average annual volume growth over previous 5 years . . .	%	1985	3.0	1.6
Gross fixed capital formation (GFCF)	% of GDP	1985	24.4	22.3
of which: Machinery and equipment	% of GDP		10.4 (84)	9.6
Residential construction	% of GDP		5.4(84)	4.6
Average annual volume growth over previous 5 years . . .	%	1984	1.9	−0.5
Gross saving ratio[4]	% of GDP	1985	20.1	24.4
General government				
Current expenditure on goods and services	% of GDP	1985	16.7	18.7
Current disbursements[5]	% of GDP	1985	33.4(84)	44.9
Current receipts	% of GDP	1985	34.1(84)	47.0
Net official development assistance	% of GNP	1984	0.46	0.28
Indicators of living standards				
Private consumption per capita using current PPP's[3] . . .	US$	1984	6 742 *	6 490
Passenger cars, per 1 000 inhabitants	Number	1985	..	306
Telephones, per 1 000 inhabitants	Number	1985	540 (83)	460
Television sets, per 1 000 inhabitants	Number	1985	..	300
Doctors, per 1 000 inhabitants	Number	1985	..	1.7
Infant mortality per 1 000 live births	Number	1985	9.2(84)	11.0
Wages and prices (average annual increase over previous 5 years)				
Wages (earnings or rates according to availability)	%	1986	7.7	5.0
Consumer prices	%	1986	8.2	3.8
Foreign trade				
Exports of goods, fob*	Million US$	1986	22 536	22 428
as % of GDP	%		14.5	33.9
average annual increase over previous 5 years	%		0.7	7.3
Imports of goods, cif*	Million US$	1986	23 916	26 724
as % of GDP	%		15.4	40.4
average annual increase over previous 5 years	%		0.1	4.9
Total official reserves[6]	Million SDR's	1986	6 202	5 778
As ratio of average monthly imports of goods	Ratio		3.7	3.0

* At current prices and exchange rates.
1. Unless otherwise stated.
2. According to the definitions used in OECD *Labour force Statistics*.
3. PPP's = Purchasing Power Parities.
4. Gross saving = Gross national disposable income *minus* Private and Government consumption.
5. Current disbursements = Current expenditure on goods and services *plus* current transfers and payments of property income.
6. Gold included in reserves is valued at 35 SDR's per ounce. End of year.
7. Including Luxembourg.
8. Included in Belgium.
9. Including non-residential construction.

EMPLOYMENT OPPORTUNITIES

Economics and Statistics Department

OECD

A. **Administrator.** A number of economist positions may become available in 1987 in areas such as monetary and fiscal policy, balance of payments, resource allocation, macroeconomic policy issues, short-term forecasting and country studies. *Essential* qualifications and experience: advanced university degree in economics; good knowledge of statistical methods and applied econometrics; two or three years' experience in applied economic analysis; command of one of the two official languages (English and French). *Desirable* qualifications and experience also include: familiarity with the economic problems and data sources of a number of Member countries; proven drafting ability; experience with the estimation, simulation and implementation of computer-based economic models; some knowledge of the other official language.

B. **Principal Administrator.** A number of senior economist positions may become available in 1987 in areas such as monetary and fiscal policy, balance of payments, resource allocation, macroeconomic policy issues, short-term forecasting and country studies. *Essential* qualifications and experience: advanced university degree in economics; extensive experience in applied economic analysis, preferably with a central bank, economics/finance ministry or institute of economic research; good knowledge of statistical methods and applied econometrics; command of one of the two official languages (English and French) and proven drafting ability. *Desirable* qualifications and experience also include: experience in using economic analysis for formulating policy advice; familiarity with a number of OECD economies; experience in using econometric models; good knowledge of the other official language.

These positions carry a basic salary (tax free) from FF 193 968 or FF 239 328 (Administrator) and from FF 275 412 (Principal Administrator), supplemented by further additional allowances depending on residence and family situation.

Initial appointment will be on a two- or three-year fixed-term contract.

Vacancies are open to both male and female candidates from OECD Member countries. Applications citing reference "ECSUR", together with a detailed curriculum vitæ in English or French, should be sent to:

> Head of Personnel
> OECD
> 2, rue André-Pascal
> 75775 PARIS CEDEX 16
> France

OECD SALES AGENTS
DÉPOSITAIRES DES PUBLICATIONS DE L'OCDE

ARGENTINA - ARGENTINE
Carlos Hirsch S.R.L.,
Florida 165, 4º Piso,
(Galeria Guemes) 1333 Buenos Aires
Tel. 33.1787.2391 y 30.7122

AUSTRALIA-AUSTRALIE
D.A. Book (Aust.) Pty. Ltd.
11-13 Station Street (P.O. Box 163)
Mitcham, Vic. 3132   Tel. (03) 873 4411

AUSTRIA - AUTRICHE
OECD Publications and Information Centre,
4 Simrockstrasse,
5300 Bonn (Germany)   Tel. (0228) 21.60.45
Local Agent:
Gerold & Co., Graben 31, Wien 1 Tel. 52.22.35

BELGIUM - BELGIQUE
Jean de Lannoy, Service Publications OCDE,
avenue du Roi 202
B-1060 Bruxelles   Tel. (02) 538.51.69

CANADA
Renouf Publishing Company Ltd/
Éditions Renouf Ltée,
1294 Algoma Road, Ottawa, Ont. K1B 3W8
Tel. (613) 741-4333
Toll Free/Sans Frais:
Ontario, Quebec, Maritimes:
1-800-267-1805
Western Canada, Newfoundland:
1-800-267-1826
Stores/Magasins:
61 rue Sparks St., Ottawa, Ont. K1P 5A6
Tel. (613) 238-8985
211 rue Yonge St., Toronto, Ont. M5B 1M4
Tel. (416) 363-3171
Sales Office/Bureau des Ventes:
7575 Trans Canada Hwy, Suite 305,
St. Laurent, Quebec H4T 1V6
Tel. (514) 335-9274

DENMARK - DANEMARK
Munksgaard Export and Subscription Service
35, Nørre Søgade, DK-1370 København K
Tel. +45.1.12.85.70

FINLAND - FINLANDE
Akateeminen Kirjakauppa,
Keskuskatu 1, 00100 Helsinki 10   Tel. 0.12141

FRANCE
OCDE/OECD
Mail Orders/Commandes par correspondance :
2, rue André-Pascal,
75775 Paris Cedex 16
Tel. (1) 45.24.82.00
Bookshop/Librairie : 33, rue Octave-Feuillet
75016 Paris
Tel. (1) 45.24.81.67 or/ou (1) 45.24.81.81
Principal correspondant :
Librairie de l'Université,
12a, rue Nazareth,
13602 Aix-en-Provence   Tel. 42.26.18.08

GERMANY - ALLEMAGNE
OECD Publications and Information Centre,
4 Simrockstrasse,
5300 Bonn   Tel. (0228) 21.60.45

GREECE - GRÈCE
Librairie Kauffmann,
28, rue du Stade, 105 64 Athens Tel. 322.21.60

HONG KONG
Government Information Services,
Publications (Sales) Office,
Beaconsfield House, 4/F.,
Queen's Road Central

ICELAND - ISLANDE
Snæbjörn Jónsson & Co., h.f.,
Hafnarstræti 4 & 9,
P.O.B. 1131 – Reykjavik
Tel. 13133/14281/11936

INDIA - INDE
Oxford Book and Stationery Co.,
Scindia House, New Delhi 1 Tel. 331.5896/5308
17 Park St., Calcutta 700016   Tel. 240832

INDONESIA - INDONÉSIE
Pdii-Lipi, P.O. Box 3065/JKT.Jakarta
Tel. 583467

IRELAND - IRLANDE
TDC Publishers - Library Suppliers,
12 North Frederick Street, Dublin 1.
Tel. 744835-749677

ITALY - ITALIE
Libreria Commissionaria Sansoni,
Via Lamarmora 45, 50121 Firenze
Tel. 579751/584468
Via Bartolini 29, 20155 Milano   Tel. 365083
Sub-depositari :
Editrice e Libreria Herder,
Piazza Montecitorio 120, 00186 Roma
Tel. 6794628
Libreria Hœpli,
Via Hœpli 5, 20121 Milano   Tel. 865446
Libreria Scientifica
Dott. Lucio de Biasio "Aeiou"
Via Meravigli 16, 20123 Milano   Tel. 807679
Libreria Lattes,
Via Garibaldi 3, 10122 Torino   Tel. 519274
La diffusione delle edizioni OCSE è inoltre
assicurata dalle migliori librerie nelle città più
importanti.

JAPAN - JAPON
OECD Publications and Information Centre,
Landic Akasaka Bldg., 2-3-4 Akasaka,
Minato-ku, Tokyo 107   Tel. 586.2016

KOREA - CORÉE
Kyobo Book Centre Co. Ltd.
P.O.Box: Kwang Hwa Moon 1658,
Seoul   Tel. (REP) 730.78.91

LEBANON - LIBAN
Documenta Scientifica/Redico,
Edison Building, Bliss St.,
P.O.B. 5641, Beirut   Tel. 354429-344425

MALAYSIA - MALAISIE
University of Malaya Co-operative Bookshop
Ltd.,
P.O.Box 1127, Jalan Pantai Baru,
Kuala Lumpur   Tel. 577701/577072

NETHERLANDS - PAYS-BAS
Staatsuitgeverij
Chr. Plantijnstraat, 2 Postbus 20014
2500 EA S-Gravenhage   Tel. 070-789911
Voor bestellingen: Tel. 070-789880

NEW ZEALAND - NOUVELLE-ZÉLANDE
Government Printing Office Bookshops:
Auckland: Retail Bookshop, 25 Rutland Street,
Mail Orders, 85 Beach Road
Private Bag C.P.O.
Hamilton: Retail: Ward Street,
Mail Orders, P.O. Box 857
Wellington: Retail, Mulgrave Street, (Head
Office)
Cubacade World Trade Centre,
Mail Orders, Private Bag
Christchurch: Retail, 159 Hereford Street,
Mail Orders, Private Bag
Dunedin: Retail, Princes Street,
Mail Orders, P.O. Box 1104

NORWAY - NORVÈGE
Tanum-Karl Johan
Karl Johans gate 43, Oslo 1
PB 1177 Sentrum, 0107 Oslo 1 Tel. (02) 42.93.10

PAKISTAN
Mirza Book Agency
65 Shahrah Quaid-E-Azam, Lahore 3 Tel. 66839

PORTUGAL
Livraria Portugal,
Rua do Carmo 70-74, 1117 Lisboa Codex.
Tel. 360582/3

SINGAPORE - SINGAPOUR
Information Publications Pte Ltd
Pei-Fu Industrial Building,
24 New Industrial Road No. 02-06
Singapore 1953   Tel. 2831786, 2831798

SPAIN - ESPAGNE
Mundi-Prensa Libros, S.A.,
Castelló 37, Apartado 1223, Madrid-28001
Tel. 431.33.99
Libreria Bosch, Ronda Universidad 11,
Barcelona 7   Tel. 317.53.08/317.53.58

SWEDEN - SUÈDE
AB CE Fritzes Kungl. Hovbokhandel,
Box 16356, S 103 27 STH,
Regeringsgatan 12,
DS Stockholm   Tel. (08) 23.89.00
Subscription Agency/Abonnements:
Wennergren-Williams AB,
Box 30004, S104 25 Stockholm.
Tel. (08)54.12.00

SWITZERLAND - SUISSE
OECD Publications and Information Centre,
4 Simrockstrasse,
5300 Bonn (Germany)   Tel. (0228) 21.60.45
Local Agent:
Librairie Payot,
6 rue Grenus, 1211 Genève 11
Tel. (022) 31.89.50

TAIWAN - FORMOSE
Good Faith Worldwide Int'l Co., Ltd.
9th floor, No. 118, Sec.2
Chung Hsiao E. Road
Taipei   Tel. 391.7396/391.7397

THAILAND - THAILANDE
Suksit Siam Co., Ltd.,
1715 Rama IV Rd.,
Samyam Bangkok 5   Tel. 2511630

TURKEY - TURQUIE
Kültur Yayinlari Is-Türk Ltd. Sti.
Atatürk Bulvari No: 191/Kat. 21
Kavaklidere/Ankara   Tel. 25.07.60
Dolmabahce Cad. No: 29
Besiktas/Istanbul   Tel. 160.71.88

UNITED KINGDOM - ROYAUME-UNI
H.M. Stationery Office,
Postal orders only: (01)211-5656
P.O.B. 276, London SW8 5DT
Telephone orders: (01) 622.3316, or
Personal callers:
49 High Holborn, London WC1V 6HB
Branches at: Belfast, Birmingham,
Bristol, Edinburgh, Manchester

UNITED STATES - ÉTATS-UNIS
OECD Publications and Information Centre,
2001 L Street, N.W., Suite 700,
Washington, D.C. 20036 - 4095
Tel. (202) 785.6323

VENEZUELA
Libreria del Este,
Avda F. Miranda 52, Aptdo. 60337,
Edificio Galipan, Caracas 106
Tel. 32.23.01/33.26.04/31.58.38

YUGOSLAVIA - YOUGOSLAVIE
Jugoslovenska Knjiga, Knez Mihajlova 2,
P.O.B. 36, Beograd   Tel. 621.992

Orders and inquiries from countries where Sales
Agents have not yet been appointed should be sent
to:
OECD, Publications Service, Sales and
Distribution Division, 2, rue André-Pascal, 75775
PARIS CEDEX 16.

Les commandes provenant de pays où l'OCDE n'a
pas encore désigné de dépositaire peuvent être
adressées à :
OCDE, Service des Publications. Division des
Ventes et Distribution. 2. rue André-Pascal. 75775
PARIS CEDEX 16.

70712-04-1987

OECD PUBLICATIONS
2, rue André-Pascal
75775 PARIS CEDEX 16
No. 44065
(10 87 28 1) ISBN 92-64-12988-X
ISSN 0376-6438

•

PRINTED IN FRANCE